the Virtual Bridge

How to Connect Remote Teams with Responsibility and Accountability

Ronald B. Beach
VIRTUAL NUGGETS SERIES

The Virtual Bridge
How to Connect Remote Teams with
Responsibility and Accountability
Copyright © 2022

For bulk order discounts, contact the publisher at:
VirtualPublishingLLC@gmail.com
111 West Trappers Loop
Chewelah, Washington 99209

Cover and Interior Design: Rebecca Finkel, FPGD.com
eBook Conversion: Rebecca Finkel, FPGD.com
Book Consultant and Editor: Judith Briles, TheBookShepherd.com

ISBN paperback: 978-1947746-13-8
ISBN paperback Ingram Spark: 978-1-947746-16-9
ISBN eBook: 978-1947746-14-5
ISBN audiobook: 978-1947746-15-2

Library of Congress Control Number: 2022903309

Business | Leadership | Remote Teams | Management

First Printing

For Larissa Meek

I can't say thank you enough to Larissa Meek, Executive Creative Director, PwC Experience Center (US). Twelve years ago, she took the time to introduce me to the world of social media and that allowed me the opportunity to reinvent myself from a manufacturing executive to that of an award-winning Amazon bestselling author, international speaker, and online college professor. Such a great example of the young teaching the old about digital trends.

Thank you, thank you, *thank you!*

Contents

Author's Note vii

CHAPTER 1 Finding Your Virtual Muscle 1

CHAPTER 2 Hiring the Best and Avoiding the
Virtual Piranha 9

CHAPTER 3 Creating Your Onboarding Process 19

CHAPTER 4 The Faces of Virtual Leadership 31

CHAPTER 5 The Power of Generations 49

CHAPTER 6 Tapping into the Creative Well 65

CHAPTER 7 Group Problem Solving Using Creativity 69

CHAPTER 8 Building the Foundation for Achievement 83

CHAPTER 9 The Right Tool to Track Performance 93

CHAPTER 10 The Pandemic Influence and Beyond 101

CHAPTER 11 My Closing Thoughts 109

Preview of Book Three: *Virtual Remote Teams* 111

About Ron Beach 115

How to Work with Ron Beach 117

Other Books by Ron Beach 119

Author's Note

What is the difference between being a member of a winning team vs a losing one? Is there a secret sauce?

Yes there is. And it's time for you to discover one of the best kept secrets in the United States, one that phenomenally successful companies in Europe and Asia embraced long ago. *Having virtual team roles is the secret sauce for workplaces today.*

In the case of the 2021 Super Bowl game, each member of the winning team will receive $150,000, according to the NFL's Collective Bargaining Agreement. Each member of the losing team will still receive $75,000, which is half the amount that the champions earn. If they only lose by one point, is that fair? Maybe not, but that is life in the football business world. Everyone remembers the winning team but can't name the team that came in second best.

The coaches of the Kansas City Chiefs and the Tampa Bay Buccaneers are all experienced leaders. All the players on the field are the best of their team. So, what is the difference?

The coaches of the winning team use each team member's individual skills and abilities in the right position. They took the time to learn each person's strengths, allowable weaknesses, what role do they perform the best in, and who each player works the best with as a partner.

The same can be found in corporate America. The highest performing teams have the right people in the right team role based on their abilities. It shouldn't be complicated, but for most companies, it has been the breaking point. A point that has eluded them.

Dr. Meredith Belbin, of Cambridge University's Henley Management College in the United Kingdom, studied teamwork for decades. He found that people who worked in ongoing successful companies were in teams. Within the teams, each participant assumed a different *team role*. Beldin believes that a team role has "a tendency to behave, contribute and interrelate with others in a particular way," and identified nine specific team roles that contributed to a team's success.

Understanding Dr. Belbin's *Team Roles Model* is a fantastic tool for teams that have become unbalanced by having too many of the same types of people on the team. Imagine if the Tampa Bay Buccaneers had an entire team in which each player was a quarterback. How about if they all had similar weaknesses? If a team has similar teamwork strengths, instead of cooperating with each other, each player may tend to concentrate on how to be competitive with his other teammates. It's a failure factor that is common in many companies today.

You'll discover the nine distinct roles of the Belbin Team Roles Model: the strengths, allowable weaknesses, and what type of team member does one work the best with.

Most leaders and managers in the United States have an understanding of the Myers-Briggs Type Indicator, but in Europe and Asia, the Belbin Team Roles Model is the management tool of choice and their leadership teams implement.

Get a cup of coffee, sit in your favorite chair, and be prepared for some interesting reading of one of the best kept secrets in the US management system—The Belbin Team Roles Model. Methods that will take you and your team from so-so to excellence.

—Dr. Ronald Beach

CHAPTER 1

Finding Your Virtual Muscle

The remote environment has forced him to expand and enhance his anticipatory skills.

The pandemic was a game changer for team leader Kyle. Before the severity of COVID strangled the workplace, working remotely was anticipated for only a few months. That was then ... this is now. The few months extended to years. Many workplaces transitioned to satellite offices from the newly dormant main offices.

Would it work?

Few workplaces were prepared for the almost instant shutdown of the traditional workplaces. The new workplace was the home.

- Did it have the bandwidth to compete with the demands of online technology?
- Did it have enough electronic equipment to meet everyone's needs?

2 The Virtual Bridge

- Did it have the space needed to homeschool noisy kids and the home workplace and the family all together 24/7?

Would the worker survive under the new normal? Would the workplace survive? Would the family survive?

> **He doesn't have a magic crystal ball.**

Kyle had survived … and he grew. He made significant strides in his remote management and communication skills, and he feels that the team is doing fantastic. With his expanded confidence and success, Kyle's areas of responsibility grew … to a level that he himself didn't think he'd ever attain.

But does his success have a dark side? Kyle is feeling he's being pulled in too many directions. The remote environment has forced him to expand and enhance his anticipatory skills—speculating a series of "what ifs." He doesn't have a magic crystal ball that he can stare into to pull answers from.

His main problems became:

- How could he keep an eye on the many little things before they became big issues?
- How should he handle a performance issue?
- When should he handle it? Are there any pitfalls that he should be alert for?
- How could he create the culture for people to take ownership of their work?

Mike was one of Kyle's remote members who was consistently missing project due dates. Think of the missed dates as being a glass with a small amount of water in it—not much to even quench any thirst. If the problem is the volume of water itself and is handled right away, it is not an issue. Contrary to the belief and practice of many, the size of the problem doesn't matter. *It's the response time.*

What is critical is how long before you see the issue and address it. If you hold the glass for an hour and don't drink, you start to feel the strain of the muscles in your arm. The small amount of water feels heavier. If you wait a day, the muscles start to become numb. The miniscule amount of water now feels like a gallon. Yet, the amount of water has not changed—the size of the problem—but it is the length of time before taking care of the issue that has become the true problem.

Kyle recognized that having to handle problems was not easy. It's not the "fun" part of the job. If given a choice, most would ignore it as much as possible, for as long as possible, hoping that it will either go away or resolve itself. Knowing that Mike was a procrastinator, Kyle created a tracking system so he, Mike, and everyone on the team could instantly see where each member was in the process. Kyle was able to back off pressure to perform and complete from his side. The other teams did it for him! They could tell that Mike's slowdowns would domino and impact them.

With all things remote, Kyle quickly learned that recognizing and handling issues—no matter how minute they seemed—was the secret to being an effective manager. It was one of the most important things he could do as a manager.

As a leader, there are three essential elements to performance issues in a virtual team that you must incorporate:

1. See the problem;

2. Address the problem; and

3. Develop a corrective action to resolve the problem.

Let's look at accountability through a different lens. Accountability has a close partner, and it is called responsibility. Think how a coin has two sides and it is nothing without the other. A football quarterback is only successful with a center to hike or pass the ball to. A company relies on customers to buy things and to pay on time.

The challenge is how to make that bridge between accountability and responsibility. On one side you have Kyle with his many different *responsibilities* and team members who are hard workers but are starting to miss important assignment due dates, one of their measurements of success where *accountability* is relevant. It's the bridge that delivers success.

If Kyle's virtual crystal ball was working, he would see Judy staring at her computer trying to get ready for his weekly team meeting. She needs to complete her status report and compile her notes for her part of the group presentation. His crystal ball would tell him that she is mentally blocked, overwhelmed from the pressures of the entire family under one roof, on top of each other in the same working area. *Will anyone be able to see how puffy my eyes are?*

She is trying to put on a good face, but her stress lines are really showing today.

Her 10-year-old son Steve is mad because her Zoom call will slow down his gaming connection. He is a great boy but having to be at home all the time has made him too connected with video games and just about anything he can manipulate electronically in the world. Her 15-year-old daughter Susan is a typical teenager who knows everything and is stressed because she has found another blemish popping up on her nose. She's convinced her virtual date tonight will think it is repulsive when he sees it.

Can't Susan stop with the moaning about her zit for a few minutes so I can get my work done?

Judy can't afford another computer, so she must balance her computer time with her husband's needing the "house" computer as well. She hopes that it won't be another night of having to stay up after everyone goes to bed to get her job done. Remember when having a good night's sleep was normal? Not in Judy's household.

Judy longs for the days of going into the office and being productive in customer meetings. Just dropping by other people's cubicles to say hi was a big part of her day. Now she is sitting in front of a screen, alone, and not feeling connected with anyone anymore. Judy understands that her work performance has taken a hit. And she knows that she is not doing her best. Some days, she feels that the stress is pushing her to the point of quitting.

I'm drowning with the virtual piranha nipping at my heels. Can I survive?

Pushing herself one more time, Judy wipes away the stress tears, puts on her faux plastic smile, and waits for the meeting to start.

WOW! Kyle has some huge challenges—yet opportunities—to really make a difference with his group. He will have to create the atmosphere for everyone to feel a part of the team. It goes beyond just setting due dates. He has the responsibility that stretches all the way back to hiring the right people, creating the culture of being part of a team in which everyone does his/her job on time, and letting any person go who isn't the right fit for the team and the work it needs to do.

It starts with:

- Hiring the right people.
- Creating an onboarding process so that new hires get into the habit of accomplishing tasks on time.
- Developing a scorecard method that helps people stay on task, creating an atmosphere for success.
- Being able to see the variety of speed bumps that life can put in the way of some people doing their jobs efficiently enough to be successful.

As a remote leader, you must get your virtual muscles ready to cross any virtual bridge.

Ron's Takeaway

Leaders and managers have a shared responsibility to provide the leadership and create a culture that supports the success of the team. They must be tuned into what the stressors are of team members that may not be instantly apparent.

7 Tips for Creating Positive Virtual Company Culture

https://www.insala.com/blog/7-tips-for-positive-virtual-company-culture. Very good blog on the dangers to employers who don't create a positive virtual culture.

5 Ways to build a strong virtual culture

https://axcient.com/blog/5-ways-to-build-a-strong-virtual-culture/.
Using Key Performance Indicators (KPIs) as the barometer for productivity gives employees the freedom to complete their work without strict policies of when and where.

Remote company culture: how to thrive with a virtual team

https://culturewise.com/blog/company-remote-team-culture/.
There are four things you can do to take a more systematic approach to manage the evolution of your company's culture.

CHAPTER 2

Hiring the Best and Avoiding the Virtual Piranha

What type of remote skill would fill in a void in your current team?

While Kyle had hired everyone in his office, he was in for a huge surprise with the challenges of hiring remote team members. His current group had been working in the office pre-COVID and their working relationships were established. If anything, he's had to hire more people and integrate into an already well-established team.

One of the surprises for "mainstream businesses" post-COVID was that a majority of those who worked remotely wanted to stay remote. Working from home has had advantages that were never envisioned. Both employers and workers discovered that overall productivity increased. The pre-COVID belief was that at-home workers would find more time for goofing-off. Instead, the at-home workers had more time to work because the commute time had disappeared. And their hour lunch break became outdated. Quick breaks would be to the kitchen for a refill of coffee. Kyle's concern now was: *Will they burn out because they are not taking the breaks they should be?*

The new work environment created an advantage for Kyle. He could seek out the best remote workers in the world, but there were disadvantages as well. He was getting bombarded with resumes from too many who were not qualified.

As a former senior director of a company, I have hired many hundreds to work in factories and a few hundred for online job openings. For the factory I would have 100 to 200 applicants for each position. My experiences with hiring for remote positions pretty much reflects what the global consulting firm for hiring *Toggl.com* found: You'll get 500 to 1,500 applications for each opening. At least 80% will be rejected right away. Do you have the time … and the energy … to go through hundreds of applicants, knowing that most are not qualified to start with? I didn't and I bet you don't either.

> **What type of remote skill would fill in a void in your current team?**

Think of the time that Kyle would need to spend on reviewing those 1,500 resumes/applications. An experienced recruiter takes an average of five to seven seconds viewing a single resume. I am a manager, not a professional recruiter, so I can afford up to 30 seconds. Recently, in my capacity as a program chair for an online university, more than 2,000 applications were received for ten online teaching positions. After going through the initial screening, 90% of the applications were discarded immediately. Of the remaining 200, it was narrowed down to 20 possibilities for the ten slots.

It sounds easy but you need to make sure you get the best people and not just people who have a good looking resume that will pass the first screening. Each could be a virtual piranha, just waiting for you to select him/her for the interview.

It's time for you to ask: What type of remote skill would fill in a void in your current team? A baseball team needs people for each position on the field. Having too many pitchers, catchers, or first basemen will not win games. Remember. You are filling an entire team.

> Is he lacking anything on his side?

Kyle needed to look at what team roles would give him that well-rounded team with backups in positions that are essential. I first introduced Kyle in my book, *The Virtual Divide*. He became familiar with the teachings of Dr. Meredith Belbin, the British leadership visionary based at Cambridge University. The Belbin Team Roles Model became Kyle's road map that catapulted his management skills to new levels.

1. **Plant:** Creative, imaginative, unorthodox, solves difficult problems.

2. **Resource Investigator:** Extrovert, enthusiastic, communicative, explores opportunities, develops contacts.

3. **Coordinator:** Mature, confident, a good chairperson, clarifies goals, promotes decision making, delegates well.

4. **Shaper:** Challenging, dynamic, thrives on pressure, has the drive and courage to overcome obstacles.

5. **Monitor Evaluator:** Sober, strategic, and discerning, sees all options, judges accurately.

6. **Team-worker:** Cooperative, mild, perceptive, and diplomatic, listens, builds, averts friction, and calms the waters.

7. **Implementer:** Disciplined, reliable, conservative, and efficient, turns ideas into practical actions.

8. **Completer:** Disciplined, dependable, focused, and efficient, turns actions into completed projects.

9. **Specialist:** Single-minded, self-starting, dedicated, provides knowledge and skills.

With his changing team, he needed to do an in-depth assessment: Was his team lacking anything in its current skills? Was he lacking anything on his side? Of the nine Belbin roles identified above, which contribution would build the team with the best chance for its continued success and sustainability?

Those who work for you have an area of interest—whether it's research, planning, or leadership—areas that they enjoy doing. They also have sub areas that they enjoy, but not to the degree of their primary interest. With the Belbin nine, someone might thrive when pressure surfaces. Another person may love to be strategic is his/her choices. Yet another person may be flexible, a great listener, and works better with calmer waters. He/she enjoys delegating.

Ideally, most teams consist of five members. If they get bigger, split the team into sub teams. Decision making becomes easier. Not surprisingly, sub teams often come up with the same results, but faster, and it gives the teams a sense of ownership.

What about you and your team? What are you looking for in the employee to strengthen the bridge that connects everyone globally?

Think about what qualities or skills that you believe the best candidate must possess and if he/she is experienced in working remotely. Ask:

- How do you manage your workload, assignments, and tasks?
- Tell me how you are about meeting deadlines on assignments?
- How do you keep yourself motivated to reach your goals?
- Do you consider yourself to be proactive or reactive?

Each of these questions requires a complete response. If there is vagueness, hesitation, or incomplete answers, you need to probe further. In addition, you need to look for how motivated he/she is along with communication skills, team interaction and collaboration with others, technical know-how, existing management and time management skills, assertiveness, plus a degree of emotional intelligence.

Skilled in Communications

For the remote workplace, topnotch communication skills would probably be the most important qualification for any successful remote employee. I would prefer to have someone who may even over-communicate rather than under-communicate when it comes to working remotely.

It is vital that someone can communicate in writing, is proficient in your language and the language that is being used within the team. Today, most international teams use English as the recognized business language of the world.

> **Anyone who has poor communication skills will struggle when working remotely.**

You want a person who is open to keeping you in the loop on the essential things, including needing time for a dental or doctor appointment that might cut into his/her work hours.

I like people who can write updates with clear, well thought out, and critical information. Too many use a lot of words to say nothing. What is needed are more people who can write with fewer words and say it all.

Anyone who has poor communication skills will struggle when working remotely. They need to have a direct, clear, professional way of speaking and writing. When I receive emails where someone writes as if it were a text message to a friend, using abbreviations, failing to use capitalization, and adding a stream of emojis … my pet peeve button is pushed.

Assertiveness

Remote workers who know when to ask questions or seek clarification move to the top of my "who do I respect" list. I have no problem with someone pushing for an answer to a question that uses polite follow-up. Kyle doesn't need a bull in the China shop. He needs someone who can be a bit pushy for an answer but not in a way that causes an HR incident.

Self-Motivated

The type of remote worker you want is someone who has the self-drive to get things done without being micromanaged.

In other words, you're looking for a person who does not need constant check-ins from the boss. In a verbal interview, be sure to include a few questions that could reveal self-reliance and self-motivation. Few resumes reveal those qualities.

Kyle does not have the time to be a "helicopter manager," making sure individuals are getting things done. It is up to the employee to make sure he/she is staying on schedule, staying to the plan and notifying the supervisor that the task is completed. Kyle's job is to be a barrier buster if the remote team member is having any issues or problems. He is a resource to help, not to do the job.

Comfortable with Technology

For remote workers, the use of technology is the door-opener in the first place. Most likely, they find your open position on a job board, which can be challenging. How comfortable are they with video conferencing and the software that will be used by the team?

The ability to write can be a challenge, especially with team members whose primary language is not yours or those of most of the team. People are so used to writing like a Twitter post and a well-meaning message can turn into a conflict in a short time. People tend to read between the lines and form their own opinions of what is being said.

Your team will likely have to work with many different video platforms so familiarity with using Skype, Slack, Zoom, and Google Teams will be valuable.

I love it when someone asks questions, and then takes the initiative to figure out where to find the answers. That might be Kyle or maybe someone else on the team.

Successful remote employees will take the time to gain new technical skills, find online tutorials and register for webinars that can help them improve their existing skills. They are not afraid of asking advice from others who may have had the same problem and resolved it.

Being Collaborative

You have the responsibility to create a positive environment where people feel comfortable working together by making your expectations clear on projects or assignments. The ability to work with others is not easily taught to a remote worker. Remote workers either have the skills and abilities, or they don't.

When you, and they, worked from an office, it was easy to get updates by talking with someone directly. Now a new hire will need to be good at knowing when to ask for a quick meeting to get help or some guidance. Working at a distance can seem that longer periods of time elapse before a question is answered or resolution arrived at. And having multiple time zones is a factor. Be aware of it.

Time Management Skills

Use of time is an indicator to me of a person's organizational skills, time management, and ability to plan. This is another pet peeve of mine: someone being late for a meeting or on assignments. That is disrespecting everyone else's time. These are all critical when working from the home environment where unplanned interruptions and distractions can be common.

Emotional Intelligence

Emotional intelligence is important in the virtual world. An emotionally intelligent worker will know when it is best to pick up a phone or have a video conference to get something solved quickly. Think of how much we rely on body language or tone of voice when we work with someone. When working remotely, the typical nonverbal communications that are visually picked up are lacking, as some of the voice tone. With emotional intelligence, an individual senses that a direct phone call is in order vs a ream of emails that transition over time.

Understanding the essential components of bringing the right people onto your team will save you hours and money. It could easily cost you ten times his/her salary if you hire the wrong person and then must find a replacement. Be smart and avoid the virtual piranha applicants. Hire the best that you can get from the beginning!

Ron's Takeaway

The savvy leader needs to know the skills of each team member. Teams should not be a "mini me" of the leader. Diversity is a plus. You hire for a diversity of skills and attitudes. But always keep in mind: You can train skills; you cannot train attitudes.

Job boards that are popular with remote workers include:

- **WeWorkRemotely** https://weworkremotely.com
- **AngelList** https://angel.co/
- **Stack Overflow** https://remote.co
- **Remote.co:** https://remote.co

CHAPTER 3

CREATING YOUR ONBOARDING PROCESS

*Employees are twice as likely to take another job
if they have a bad onboarding experience.*

Most managers know what Kyle will experience ... onboarding new hires is hard work. Why? Because it sets the stage for long-term good or bad performances.

Since 2005, the number of people working remotely has increased 159%, according to Upwork's "Future of Workforce Pulse Report" in September 2020. By 2025, 36.2 million Americans will be working remotely. This is an 87% increase from pre-pandemic levels.

Companies like Dell host all onboarding materials on a dedicated website. Stack Overflow sets up phone calls between the new hires and executives to answer questions. Why should you care? Simply this: Employees are twice as likely to take another job if they have a bad onboarding experience. By creating a solid plan, you can save time, money, and having to retrain replacements.

There are many make or break parts of this virtual bridge that include:

- Giving the new hire confidence and making him/her feel welcome.
- Developing the foundation of a strong relationship with others in the company.
- Helping new hire understand the culture and how work must be delivered on time.
- Setting clear expectations and how he/she will support the organization's mission, vision, and goals.
- Making each new employee feel part of a much larger team and seen as valuable to its success.

Too many organizations make the mistake of using the same onboarding plan for remote new hires as they did with face-to-face hires. There are some similarities but some necessary changes to the approach of onboarding remote new hires. The method that Kyle used to hire was exclusively face to face. No longer is that the norm, especially in the virtual world.

The biggest barrier to creating a great onboarding experience is often the acceptance of the manager's responsibility to set the stage to help the employee understand his/her accountability as a team member.

Getting off to a positive start and a sense of belonging.

Think back to the first day in your last job. I bet that you didn't sleep very well, unsure of the expectations and the butterflies as you wondered if you could really do the job. Think about your anticipation, the doubt you may have had that you may not have the full skillset needed—that what you wrote you could do made you feel like an imposter. And, of course, the general uncertainty that surrounds a job application and magnify this even more when the new position is a virtual one. Did you feel isolated, not sure who to turn to for feedback, questions, or just checking in? Working virtually can be a lonely number. Some thrive on it; some struggle to exist.

When I was the senior director in manufacturing for LSI Logic, I would take all new hires to lunch and get to know them better. And my goal was to settle their nerves. A manager's lunch with a new employee is outdated for most and nonexistent for the virtual world, unless you Zoom lunch together at the same time, which I do.

Most of time, I'm on the phone or a video call connecting and striving to let them understand that they are not alone. We have all been there and will be their partner. And, that I am available, although remotely. Obviously, the power of seeing a casual smile or that sense of belonging was much easier in the office.

> **Pay me now or pay me later.**

Kyle knows that he must keep the elements of virtual onboarding in mind. He starts by developing a plan to leverage different strategies that will bypass the speed bumps and help the employee feel welcome. When the new hire feels welcome, his/her confidence grows. Any uncertainty of joining Kyle and the team evaporates. The new hire made the right decision to join you and the team.

From the beginning, you need to communicate that *you will be* the dedicated onboarding connection. Many feel that they just don't have the time to do the hand-holding many new employees need. They are wrong. They, and you, can't afford not to. Having had my feet in both the traditional working world for decades and now in the virtual world for over 15 years, this is the reality: The time invested now will save you many headaches in the future. It is the adage: "Pay me now or pay me later."

Kyle's "pay now" strategy included:

1. Holding weekly one-on-ones with new hires to check in and offer support.
2. Having a video group meeting so everyone on the team can meet each other.
3. Making sure all understood that his virtual door was open.
4. Converting any hard copy training manuals, employee handbooks, and procedure packets and forwarding them. In addition, making sure that they can access any of these documents through an online employee portal.
5. Having training videos and learning modules that the new hire can complete. The result was that it eased up Kyle's time and he could monitor progress.

Here's one more idea that I carried over from my brick and mortar days. For new members of my teams, I send a *welcome package* to their home before their first day on the team. It could be samplings of the company's products, restaurant gift cards, Amazon cards, or if something had been revealed in their interview that they engaged in and liked, plus a personal congratulations note. I want them to feel that I only select the best of the best and they need to know that.

Set up technology before the start date.

Offer each person a session with your tech support team on how the company systems work. Videos of how the video conferencing platform works or tricks on how to use them would be a good starting point.

Some companies send their new employees a laptop or phone before their start date that's already set up for the connections to the company's configurations and security protocols. If this is one of your policies, let your new hires know to expect it and be sure to ask what address they would like it sent to.

On your list are several important needs to be supplied:

- Wi-Fi capacity
- Use logins and company access
- Security guidelines
- Virtual Private Network (VPN) needs
- Licensed company software

- Noise-canceling headphones
- Webcam and access to video conferencing sites used by the company

Making strong relationships with others in the organization.

The virtual workplace can sometimes be very lonely, and new hires can feel adrift, not connected to anything, and surrounded by the virtual piranha, just nipping at their feet.

A checklist of one-on-one connections is a significant tool to have and use. It not only lets new hires feel how they are a part of a much larger team but to help answer any of the tons of questions floating in their minds. It is easy for many to work by themselves, but it takes time to develop those relationships with others who could be of assistance or provide valuable support. To do this, formal and informal experiences help them build that virtual community, the virtual community that is now their team.

Building on those one-on-one connections. For example, a phone call with a Human Resources representative could help cover rules and responsibilities. These calls are much like those that would take place in an office visit. Video conferencing has the advantage of taking the place of the office visit and is easy to schedule.

Use team dynamics to build that new hire's network.
By designing your checklist early, leaders can help build a powerful network. In my checklist, I also include being part of team discussions so they can get past the fear of what leadership is like. My goal is to view myself as a *fly on the wall*, but I'm also viewing my own interactions with team members.

- Do I shoot the messengers that come from team members?
- Do I interrupt them when they are speaking or exchanging information?
- Do I practice the art of listening?
- Is there a level of trust and rapport in the team?
- How does the work get completed?

According to the Society of Human Resource Management, employee turnover can be as much as 50% in the first 18 months of employment. The onboarding experience can play an incredibly significant role in keeping those new employees for the long-term by setting them up for success.

This is the perfect time to set the stage for the expectations of how any new hires will interact with you and what your expectations are. I have a weekly one-on-one phone call just to check on how he/she is doing with the onboarding process and get to know person better. Does the new hire have children? Ask about any hobby interests right now and/or favorite things to do.

Each week, I hold a virtual conference with all the new hires together. The key thing is to show how others are in the same boat. I like to keep it very lighthearted and work to feel that every question is a great one since others may be wondering also. *Are they experiencing a roadblock that I can help with?* This shows how I will work with them as a resource and have their back. More than half of employees report experiencing a mishap during onboarding. It could be not having the required technology, not having a company overview, missing coworker introductions, etcetera. And I don't record them. My experience was that members were quieter and non-participatory when I did.

Be sure to give your new hires time to review training videos, documents, complete their human resources orientation, sign their documents, and learn about benefits. Plus, provide them with an organizational chart. For years, I scratched my head as to why companies don't share them with employees … as if they want to keep these things under wraps. It was an HR executive who stopped my head from the itch when he shared, "We stopped producing organizational charts when we discovered that executive headhunters were trolling our public information to recruit our key people." I got it.

Finally, give them a calendar of events, or anything else that your team uses daily.

Show them how the company culture works to get things done.

Your position should be: We don't keep secrets. Every company has its own culture on how things are done. It should not be a secret and you can bring new hires into the loop during your weekly phone calls. You want them to feel comfortable enough to ask questions about how things work on the team as well as with the company overall.

Assign a buddy. If you are hiring an exceptionally large group of people at one time, maybe your calendar can only handle so many meetings. Assign someone on each team as the culture buddy who can function as a guide and lamp post of how things should or should not be done.

Milestones do count. In your checklist, set specific milestones to be completed and how to measure their effectiveness in the onboarding process. What you want to show is how you expect achievement of them and open communication on any issue. That sets the stage of showing how speed bumps are normal but can be navigated: under, over, around, or through.

> **Help them feel that they are part of something special.**

Your online employees expect training. Did you realize that 67% of remote workers are looking for more work-related training, according to recent studies. Give them the opportunity to access online courses during or after their orientation. How about including a small stipend for their professional development? Either for specific courses or to be a type of "bank" that a set amount can be drawn down on? I give certificates for free technical training to an online computer store. They got the training I felt was needed, and they were able to add something to their resume. That satisfies the "What is in it for me" as well as "What is in it for them."

Help them feel that they are part of something special. Send them links to company articles, videos, and some swag or a perk occasionally.

Set clear expectations and connect with your regular operation of the team.

New hires should have a clear picture in their mind of your view of success and what is expected of them in their first few months. Every ... one ... of ... them. I normally tell them that my expectations for the first year is to learn how things work, how to be part of the team, and can be relied upon to meet deadlines. That's the first year ... nothing more.

Then there's forward. In the second year is when I expect them to be able to be contributors to the team's goals and objectives, to grow the value of the team and of the work we do.

This monitoring of their progress helps you keep an eye on how they are doing, how comfortable they are with the organization, and how they manage the objectives. This is where honest and detailed feedback is critical. You want to acknowledge the things that they are doing right and offer support for those that are not doing so well. The key is that you are showing your expectations of achievement and ability to accomplish goals on time or to ask for some help.

Remember ... your new hires must know their responsibilities and how to prioritize items for quick wins that create that solid foundation for their success. The goal is for you to use the onboarding process as a method of showing how you set goals, expect results, communicate, are willing to be a resource, and will work with them toward their success.

Ron's Takeaway

Onboarding is at the top of the essential list. It's key and sets the stage for what your expectations are. Be consistent. Present them with clarity. And make sure that all new hires understand their role on the team and what exactly is expected of them.

Remote employees onboarding checklist resources:

- workable *https:workable.com*
- indeed.com *https://www.indeed.com*

CHAPTER 4

The Faces of Virtual Leadership

Those who manage today with a dinosaurian attitude and methodology will become extinct ... replaced by the new leader who combines both leadership and management traits.

All leaders have two main roles in an organization: to simulate creativity and innovation, and to urge participation and achievement. They are the two sides of the same managerial coin. The same goes for the leadership style used in a virtual team—that of being a leader as well as a manager. The question becomes: *What are the faces of the virtual leader?*

Contrary to belief, leading a virtual team is harder than a regular office job ... much harder. That's because you must be able to shift styles of leadership based on the situation, the type of projects, along with the stress and attitudes of the team members. Yes, you do all the things within the traditional office, but there are essential elements missing. The ability to quickly deal with something versus having to set a schedule to "discuss" issues across multiple time zones creates barriers. Not seeing everyone at the same time—the body languages, the voice tones and the level of the tones—creates more barriers.

This challenge is also what makes the virtual leader much more valuable to a company. He or she needs chameleon features, i.e., the ability to deal with and adapt to change influenced by his/her surroundings.

Not only must you continually change your leadership style, but you also don't have the luxury of assuming the role like you would typically do in a physical office with others. The higher level executives are more like the managers—setting goals, targets, and objectives. The leaders implement and run the daily operations, accomplishing those goals and targets by collaborating and working with their people. You must be able to do either at any time and shift your role quickly. With the combination of both the traditional office manager and leader, the virtual "new" leader moves light years ahead of the traditional office leaders as far as what responsibility is. But with that responsibility comes a new type of fun … the "fun" of being the captain of your own team. The virtual leader's face also brings autonomy.

The leader vs the manager role

Some feel that leaders are people who do the right things and managers are people who do things right. Another way of saying it is that managers get other people to do a job, while leaders get it done by getting people to want to do it.

Leaders are interested in direction, vision, goals, objectives, intention, purpose, and effectiveness—the right things. Managers are more interested in efficiency, the how-to, the day-to-day, the short run of doing things right.

In my early years as a supervisor, I used Warren G. Bennis' list of distinctions he identified in *On Becoming a Leader*. I adapted his variances between a manager and a leader as a foundation of developing my own personal leadership style. Bennis has thirteen. I modified them to become the foundation of what I've taught and used in workshops for decades. My eight are:

> **The manager asks why and how; the leader asks what and why.**

- A manager administers; the leader innovates.
- The manager is a copy; the leader is an original.
- The manager maintains; the leader develops.
- The manager focuses on systems and structure; the leader focuses on people.
- The manager relies on control; the leader inspires trust.
- The manager has a short-term view; the leader has a long-term view.
- The manager asks why and how; the leader asks what and why.
- The manager has an eye on the bottom line; the leader has an eye on the horizon.

Leading a Virtual Team

Every leader has his/her own set of specific "tools" … the go to, must-have … successful leader's toolbox. The leaders that I've consistently observed always start with the big picture and share it. The teaching includes:

- Create a shared vision.
- Ensure customer satisfaction.
- Live the values.
- Build teamwork.
- Think globally.
- Appreciate cultural diversity.
- Empower people.
- Anticipate opportunity.
- Achieve competitive advantage.
- Embrace change.
- Share leadership.
- Demonstrate personal mastery.
- Show technological savvy.
- Encourage constructive challenge.

It is important to note how corporate vision, customer satisfaction and values are at the top of the list. Each alone is non-measurable, but the inclusion for success is easily understood.

What if you ignore the warning signs?

The ostrich factor is the norm in too many environments. Many managers take the position that if they ignore the signals that define tomorrow's reality, the problems will eventually go away. They don't. If anything, they simmer, then beginning seeding more. The problems end up creating more. This attitude and belief of "it will go away" supports the concept that change is doing what has always been done. Therefore, tighter control, ever more aggressive micromanagement, and deeper cost cutting is necessary. This belief, hide it and it will go away, has led many teams to failure. That failure may come quickly or take a longer period, but failure will still occur.

Change leadership

Successful leaders who thrive when change is in play do not favor either a top-down or bottom-up thinking, nor do they compromise by using bits of each. Instead, the best strategy is to pursue both in combination. By that, the organization does not have to compromise. It gets the best of both. Survey data suggest that a truth, trust, love, and collaboration approach is unlikely to succeed so other methods are needed to get the support of the rank and file. What they do favor is the strength of group dynamics and the need to understand how teams progress through change.

Change at the team level

Work teams have been deeply ingrained in our society since our earliest stages of history. Drawings in caves reflect how early man formed hunting teams to survive. The ancient Egyptians built their pyramids using workers who were skilled in building pyramids. The ancient Chinese built the Great Wall of China by the efforts of peasants. And the Romans constructed aqueducts and Hadrian's Wall. The soldiers became builders during times when war ceased. In fact, without the use of manufacturing teams, our country would not be in the advanced world position of leadership that it now enjoys.

This background has laid the foundation for the forward-looking manager to utilize in any corporate change project. Those who manage today with a dinosaurian attitude and methodology will become extinct ... replaced by the new leader who will combine both leadership and management traits.

Teamwork is one of the most common prescriptions for coping with change. Typical benefits with the team approach are breaking down barriers to effective communications and collaboration, increasing the speed of action, and raising the level of commitment. Additional team approach benefits include creating a more customer-focused culture and increasing organizational adaptability and flexibility. Jobs that require flexible and innovative behavior are ingrained with a degree of constant change that may provide a higher level of job satisfaction.

> **Change is here to stay. And without it, you stagnate in your growth as a leader.**

Today's workers are more skilled and more educated and more demanding about their role in the workplace. They have higher aspirations levels; have a greater need for personal development and growth; and have a greater need for personal time and leisure. Also, they face more job changes in a lifetime compared to previous generations and have a different concept of loyalty.

The ability to change is the key to unlock a remote team's survival, although as managing change is commonly thought of last. But it is one of the most critical roles of a leader!

The sad part is so few are as successful as they could be. The concept of organizational change is no longer an exclusive tool used only by the larger corporations. More than 80% of American companies are now undergoing at least one major business change. Change is here to stay. And without it, you stagnate in your growth as a leader.

Transformational Leadership

Transformational leadership is all in the key word: *transform*. As the leader, you create an atmosphere where your team can embrace an evolvement attitude and experience—the cocoon to the butterfly.

The strength of this method is that it is a specific skillset, and your personal charisma is one of those connecting factors. Charismatic leaders can get people to move beyond their own wants to a level that they strive for the benefit of the team. Your skillset includes being proactive, change-oriented, innovative, motivating, and inspiring, and having a vision or mission. You infuse the group … delivered with your insight and yes, your charisma. Your people will respond with a stronger commitment and a bonding and loyalty to the group.

Transformational leaders create a positive relationship with their people in such a way that the team functions with improved performance. I've always used a combination of direct emails and phone calls during the week with each team member ... outside of team meetings. It reinforces both inspiration and motivation.

Transactional Leadership

Transactional leadership's key word is *action*. It assumes that the virtual leader and team member influence the results so that each gets something of value. Think of it as the carrot and stick approach ... if you do this ... you get that. Another way of describing it is that a leader gives their employees something they want in exchange for something the leader needs. This creates a relationship of mutual dependence in which the contributions of both sides are acknowledged and rewarded. This is the leadership concept that closely aligns with results that can be considered as win-wins.

Transactional leadership is when the leader sees possibilities that can come from working together. The transactional manager's reward-leadership style clarifies expectations and offers recognition when goals are achieved. The clarification of goals and objectives and providing recognition once goals are achieved should result in individuals and teams achieving expected levels of performance.

Transactional management-by-exception leadership is comprised of two separate factors: setting goals and acknowledging results. In a more active form of active management by exception, the transactional leader sets the targets, as well as defining what would be considered unsatisfactory performance, and may punish the team for failing to meet the goal. This style of leadership implies closely monitoring for deviances, mistakes, and errors and then taking corrective action as quickly as possible if any occur.

In its more passive form, the transactional leader waits until a crisis arises before acting—or takes no action at all. It would be called p*assive-avoidant* or *laissez-faire*. Such passive leaders avoid clarifying expectations or providing goals and standards to be achieved by followers.

There is a yin and yang view for the two.

Transformational leadership looks to reward. Transactional leadership looks to correct.

Servant Leadership

The final leadership style is one that Robert K. Greenleaf revealed in his book *Servant Leadership*. His pioneering book became the inspiration for a new type of leadership: servant leadership. Originally, bookstores placed it in the religious section for shelving. Today, it is considered the core of leadership philosophy and methods. He believed that leadership must, primarily, meet the needs of others. Leadership expert Stephen Covey said of Greenleaf's enlightened work,

> The servant leadership concept is a principle, a natural law, and getting our social value systems and personal habits aligned with this ennobling principle is one of the great challenges of our lives.

The primary goal of servant leadership is that a leader's first responsibility is to serve the organization, as a fundamental linkage between leaders and their people.

My involvement with leadership started with the hardcore thoughts and techniques learned from my time as a sergeant in the Marines and then a cop where an authoritative style was embraced. After leaving the Marines, I became a plant manager with Hitachi, where transformational techniques were ingrained—a vastly different influence from the authoritative styles of the military. My leadership knowledge was further expanded when I became a director at LSI Logic where I crossed over and became a servant leader. Servant leadership changed the overall emphasis of the company's goals to one that served the employees … meeting their goals and objectives.

> **Service is the core of servant leadership. Leaders' egos are set aside.**

My personal growth that has become the core of my teachings was reinforced with the guidance of Kenneth Melrose's book *Making the Grass Greener on Your Side: A CEO's Journey to Leading by Serving*. His belief in and ability to connect with people, make tough decisions, and his commitment to quality and innovation, led Toro to record results. Turning the financially strapped Toro Lawn Mower Company around became his mission.

> Everyone has the potential to contribute to achieving the goals of the company. If you unleash that potential, market leadership and financial success will be natural byproducts.

His use of the servant leadership style empowered him to see the job through and guided it through tough times, and greater heights of success. The turnaround and success came without him seeking personal recognition or accolades. It was all about highlighting the employees as the key to what was accomplished during his tenure.

The fundamental motivation for leadership should be a desire to serve their followers.

- Servant leadership is not about lack of direction but about implementation.
- Servant leaders highly value human equality and seek to enhance the personal development and professional contributions of all organizational members.
- Servant leaders give up personal rights to find greatness in service to others.

Servant Leadership Attributes

If servant leadership is different from other forms of leadership, then one should be able to observe characteristics and behaviors in such leaders that are distinctive. Service is the core of servant leadership. Leaders' egos are set aside. Service in leadership has a moral imperative. The leaders who do choose a service role set about providing the resources others need to achieve success. They serve by making information available, and share their time, attention, material that give meaning to the work.

Larry Spears, the former executive director of the Greenleaf Center for Servant Leadership, in his book *On Becoming a*

Servant Leader reveals his 10 critical characteristics of the servant leader:

1. **Listening:** Servant leaders must reinforce these important skills by making a deep commitment to listening intently to others.

2. **Empathy:** The most successful servant leaders are those who have become skilled empathetic listeners.

3. **Healing:** Kenneth Greenleaf wrote in *Servant Leadership*: "There is something subtle communicated to one who is being served and led if implicit in the compact between servant leader and led is the *understanding that the search for wholeness is something they share.*"

4. **Awareness:** Able leaders are usually sharply awake and reasonably disturbed.

5. **Persuasion:** Reliance upon persuasion, rather than positional authority.

6. **Conceptualization:** To be a servant leader, thinking must be stretched to encompass broader-based conceptual thinking. There is a delicate balance between conceptualization and day-to-day focus.

7. **Foresight:** The ability to foresee the likely outcome of a situation is hard to define, but easy to identify. It is deeply rooted within the intuitive mind. *Foresight is the one servant leader characteristic with which one may be born.* Greenleaf proposed foresight to be the central ethic of leadership.

8. Stewardship: Holding something in trust for another.

9. Commitment to the growth of people: Belief that people have an intrinsic value beyond their tangible contributions as workers.

10. Building community: Servant leaders seek to identify a means for building community among those who work within a given institution.

As someone who transitioned from the common authoritarian model of most US companies to today's employee-focused and more successful business, I've learned that.

1. *Measuring success must have communication and interpersonal interaction in its mix.* Think of it as looking for four parts praise to one part constructive criticism. And managers are expected to have at least one "coaching session" with a staff member, peer, or supervisor each month.

2. *Creating expectations*: If a manager has an up-to-date and clear performance expectation for each departmental goal and team members feel that they have the resources they need to meet those expectations, this management expectation has been met.

3. *Last, but by no means least, a successful leader says, "Thanks!"* Managers meet this expectation when they write at least one thank you note each week, give at least two "thank yous" each week to people who don't report to them, and verbally thank everyone on every shift.

What Does It All Mean?

The role of the 21st century leader must be one in which he/she establishes the vision and communicates it in a way that helps people link their day-to-day work with the organization's strategic objectives. The leadership style must be one that shapes values. The leader must be the supporter, resource provider, obstacle remover, facilitator, consultant, and team builder. Only when this can be accomplished will the full potential of an organization be realized.

It is not that one style of leadership is better than another. Each has a place and time for use. Researchers use too broad of a paintbrush when it is presented that only one model is acceptable over another. Even Greenleaf, who coined the phrase servant leadership in 1970, believed that the leader-first and the servant-first are two extreme types. Between them there are shadings and blends that are part of the infinite variety of human nature. With the rapidly changing business environment, the 21st century virtual leader must be able to change his/her leadership style to match the situation. In fact, earlier research on transformational leadership has shown that it augments transactional leadership in predicting performance.

> Servant leaders realize that their followers do not work for them. They work for the followers.

Transformational leaders motivate followers to accept and meet difficult goals that they would not have attempted. This is adopted when the followers, thereby changing their attitudes, beliefs and personal goals, adopt the leader's values.

Servant leadership is more than just making the goals clear and then rolling your sleeves up and doing whatever it takes to help people win. Servant leaders realize that their followers do not work for them. They work for the followers. Leaders who model servant leadership must see their employees from a unique perspective. Because each person has a deep hunger to be recognized, valued, appreciated, and understood, the employee needs to be perceived as having an intrinsic value that extends beyond just being a corporate asset.

A company should consider a period long enough to make major shifts in its organization's direction, but not so long as to seem meaningless. Generally, small groups that operate in quickly changing environments plan two to three years into the future. A three to 10 year perspective is more common for larger organizations that may require a longer lead time to make major changes.

When this is combined with the short-term improvement activities of the transactional leader, it is understandable why the changes fail to remain effective. The objective is not long-term growth, but short-term gain. The CEO and board of directors are successful, but the actual result is that the organization is paying a very heavy price. Most companies consider their "stakeholders" as their stock shareholders. They aren't. True stakeholders are your employees … the ones that will grow a company with the leader's guidance.

Regardless of which leadership style is used, care must be taken so that the goals and objectives are clear to the followers. Too many times the message is sent that everything is important. *Everything is not important.* New initiatives are started without stopping other activities, or too many initiatives are started at the same time.

The result is massive overwhelm. They overwhelm, overload, and disorient the very people who need to take responsibility for the work. To the follower, this is more like a theory of the week concept. And if they ignore it long enough, everything will return to the previous norm.

All three forms of leadership have a common thread of leadership and it is call ethics. This leadership consists of three segments:

1. the moral character of the leader.
2. the ethical legitimacy of the values embedded in the vision that the followers will either embrace or reject; and
3. the morality of the processes of social ethical choice and action that the leaders and their people engage in and collectively pursue.

The challenge for tomorrow is to lead by example today. Keep in mind that any manager and leader—virtual or onsite—can dictate an organization to be mediocre, but they will only get world-class performance if they get employees to want it as badly as they do.

CHAPTER FOUR: The Faces of Virtual Leadership 47

Ron's Takeaway

Situation leadership is the secret sauce for leadership success and using the correct leadership theory for the time, the situation, and corporate culture you work in. You must be willing to change as the results do. Change is the only constant.

Seven strategies for virtual change management are revealed on the How Space website: *https://www.howspace.com*.

1. Start with the why
2. Invite all stakeholders to help build the strategy
3. Cocreate
4. Give everyone a voice
5. Facilitate, don't dictate
6. Be transparent and agile
7. Leverage the right digital tools

CHAPTER 5

THE POWER OF GENERATIONS

Global competition will eliminate the survival of companies that depend solely on and practice what made them successful over the last twenty years.

Kyle is now at the point of tackling the issues of the post COVID-19 virtual workplace. Four generations are in play: the first consists of managers approaching retirement; the next is moving into the executive ranks; the third into management and supervisory roles; the fourth is moving into the workforce.

Interesting, confusing, and upheaval at times, this combination could result in one tremendously successful blending or one of the most traumatic social impacts of our century. Conflict between generations is inevitable and virtual leaders must understand how these distinct groups will continue to have differing opinions and colliding cultural and social values.

The demands for more products, shorter lead times, lower cost and zero defects are creating pressure on the manufacturing managers to understand the differences in management styles that will have to be utilized to reach their organization's maximum potential. While this is one of the toughest elements for virtual leaders, they must understand the generational strengths and weaknesses so they can be a valuable part of their teams.

What are the generations?

We are at a time where there are four unique generations at play. Values are different. Company loyalties are different. Attitudes are different. Lifestyles are different. Workplace tools are different. Communication styles are different. Socialization is different. Family life is different. Customer service is different.

There is the Generation Z, 1996 to present; Millennial generation (also called Gen Y), 1977–1995; Generation X, 1965–1976; and the Baby Boomers, 1946–1964. Each can be looked at as having its own special characteristics. With those differences in mind, the virtual leader must contend with the conflicts and rethink how each must be led and managed in several ways. Each has a variety of strengths that a forward-looking leader will realize and blend into an effective virtual group.

The generations defined by name, birth year, and ages in 2022 is based on widespread consensus by the Beresford Research Group. They are the birth years and ages of the generations you'll want to use post-2021 until the NEXT generation identifier is identified. And the name of it rarely sticks until it is unfolding.

	Born	Ages	Size
TBA	2022–?		
Gen Z	1997–2021	1–24	67.1 million
Millennails	1981–1996	25–40	72.3 million
Gen X	1965–1980	41–56	64.9 million
Boomers II	1955–1964	57–66	70.7 million
Boomers I	1946–1954	67-75	
Silent	1928–1945	76–93	20.9 million
Greatest	before 1928	94–99	1.7 million

The Boomers generation is occasionally broken up into two distinct groups because the span is so large, and the older group has different sensibilities and viewpoints than the younger one. In the US, Boomers II are just young enough to have missed being drafted into the Vietnam War.

There are several names for Generation X: Twenty something's, baby busters, grunge kids, and slackers. Gen X has tags as the 13th Generation, loser generation, malcontents, lazy, yuppies, 13ers, the lost generation, whiners, underachievers, yiffies, the doofus generation, the nowhere generation, the latchkey generation, the helicopter parent generation. It is unfortunate since all of these give such a negative connotation to one of the most exciting and formative generations to come along.

Today's managers are at a crucial crossroad.

Gen Xers were born when the country was experiencing soaring prices, wage inflation, stagnant consumer demands, and increased unemployment. They saw their parents stay with a single employer for decades only to be laid off. The financial and emotional turmoil that followed imprinted their attitudes and behaviors, setting the stage for the ideologies that will surface later: some good; others not so good. Inflation forced more dual income families and higher divorce rates. While they are characterized as being pragmatic and cynical realists, this generation is thought to be more global, technologically oriented, and more culturally diverse then previous generations. Gen Xers are likely to be the first generation to fail to match their parents' economic success.

The Baby Boomers is one of tremendous size—a size that fueled significant changes in society, technology, and living. They spawned much of our nation's current culture and economy. They value creativity, love adventure, seek independence, are risk takers and expanded the economy more than any previous generation. In fact, their dedication and drive to improve their economic standings is one of the very items that made it possible for Gen X to be what it is today. The ways in which the youth of Gen X were raised are an important fiber of the thread of their inner drives. Unfortunately, they are greatly misunderstood and unappreciated for their full potential.

> **Trade schools and "votech" ... vocational technology will be bubbling up.**

The Gen X worker has been painted as being bored, unmotivated, unwilling to read, refusing to study, rude and who felt not only entitled to A's and B's but demanded them.

There are positive traits that need to be considered. While fewer in number, they are more diverse, techno literate, and crave attention. And while being impatient, they have a strong curiosity and are fearless in being independent and self-reliant.

There are others who feel that Gen X should be considered as being cautious, independent, and comfortable with change. This is the group that embraced "job hopping." Loyalty to the employer and workplace wasn't the core that their parents believed in. Researchers predicted that in the workplace of the future, corporations would be looking for the young people who were suited for flexible, high performance work environments that were riddled with change. This seems to match the shift in remote organizations to that of work teams requiring a more diverse set of skills and being able to assume more responsibility as management layers become flatter and leaner.

There are significant influences that serve as the root of Gen X. The dissolution of the traditional nuclear family is a strong one. Gen X is the first generation in which mothers were on the pill and where divorce was common. Some 40% have grown up in broken families. And some see Gen Xers as the children of neglect.

Unlike the other generations, Gen Z has had to inherit a post COVID-19 virtual workplace that has also reshaped the social and economic landscape, delivering an uncertain future. They are on track to be the best-educated generation yet, less likely to drop out of high school and the highest of the generations enrolled in a two-year or four-year college. Gen Z is more likely to have a college educated parent than previous generations of young people. While they are just entering the workforce, don't count them out. And don't let them fall off your radar screen.

> Most basic core beliefs will have to change.

Post COVID-19, the projection is that there will be less university level education with a new emphasis on specific skills. That means trade schools and "votech" … vocational technology will be bubbling up. Yes, we're talking about the same schools and skills that were routinely taught and encouraged when the Baby Boomers were in elementary and high schools being prevalent again.

Corporate Culture

Today's managers are at a crucial crossroad. One direction management could take leads to accelerated movement toward an organization that allows managers to use a wide spectrum of managerial approaches and the ability for flexibility in their execution. The other course leads to the concept of the more continued slow, and sometimes resistant, movement that only maintains the status quo.

Global competition will eliminate the survival of companies that depend solely on what made them successful over the last twenty years.

Although changes will be hard for management to accept, most core beliefs will have to change. One is the adage that the ability to conceal information was power. While that may have been true in the past, the future says *that true power* will be had by allowing that same information to become common knowledge and available to their general workforce.

Managers who still hold information close to their chest are stifling one of the greatest resources that the different generations of workers can bring to the table. Their inner need for information is such a strong driving force that it is the center for almost everything they do. Consider how Gen Xers have grown up being exposed to massive amounts of television, which has gone to the point of instant world communications. If they have a question, they can jump on the internet to satisfy almost any matter that comes to mind. Companies are spending massive amounts of capital investment dollars to expand their computer networks to give information to a larger band of workers.

In a time of these great technological advances, the Generation X worker has benefitted greatly over the previous generations. They are techno literate and enjoy technology-driven jobs. Combining this with the desire for up-to-date information and the tools to connect with it, the manager has a requirement to develop and supply highly scannable training materials that will be an eye-catching, visually pleasing experience for the Gen X worker. This need generates a demand for corporations to provide continuous and enriching education. If it doesn't, the Gen X employee will jump ship in a nanosecond. Think w*hat's in it for me (WIIFM)*. This is a motto that the Gen Xer embraces.

Management Trends

It must be understood that there are distinct differences among the generations. To maintain a steady workforce, the companies of today must strive to make it where employees want to be.

The Gen X employees have different motivations that need to be understood and planned for. The Xers are twice as likely to remain with an employer due to compensation and more likely to leave for higher salary. And the Boomers may not be happy with their salary, but they are less likely to leave.

Education and Training

While corporations may offer some sort of educational support, the future will demand that more flexible policies will need to be in place to prepare the ever-drying-up entry workforce with some of the basic foundations of an education. To the shock of most businesses, those applying for entry level positions lack the most basic skills in reading and writing, nor can solve problems that previous generations were typically taught. This reflects a strong discrepancy between the education being supplied and the lack of applicable skills being taught that are holding back young people from getting into the job market.

> The savvy manager must recognize who has what; who needs help; and what methods would be best to use for each.

The impact on the workplace is significant. The dominoing factor is in play: from the quality of work, the loss of productivity, the loss of profits, which results in loss of jobs. The scope of tuition reimbursement, allowance for paid time-off to finish essential certifications and/or degrees and in supplying more inhouse seminars, workshops, and training could and should be expanded.

The improved results in the education of all generations give them more of an ability to keep up with the rapid technology advances that managers are seeing daily. Not only are young technical savvy people needed to maintain current systems, but we will also need uniquely suited qualities for those forward-looking companies that are advancing into the future. The reality is that all generations have learned assets and skills businesses need. The savvy manager must recognize who has what; who needs help; and what methods would be best to use for each.

Future Trends

The changing composition of the workforce: it's more educated, but is it educated in the right places? The workforce is more female, often part of a two-earner family, and more likely to include members of a minority group. The workforce is aging, which poses challenges to the traditional modes of compensation and organization of work schedules.

> The combo of traditional workplace and the virtual workplace—whether it's global or across town—will be the new norm.

The vast array of blending of the generations will be a strong influence on managers and those they work with. Getting things done will take more politics, planning, education, problem solving and quicker solutions to problems. The shift will be more to reflect a strong drive for work-life balance. This, combined with single parent households in the workforce with women and minorities being the largest percentage of new workers. There will be a push for shorter workweeks enhanced by improved productivity supported by technology.

The idea of the solo brick and mortar will be outdated. The combo of traditional workplace and the virtual workplace—whether it's global or across town—will be the new norm.

Gen X and Strategic Planning

There are three main factors for virtual leaders of Generation X that will have to be considered:

1. The use of common sense,
2. The use of empowerment, and
3. The use of an open-door policy.

The companies that teach managers to use common sense will attract the best of the best. Companies must plan to develop their employees' skills and abilities, along with management on how to manage when there are differences of generational styles. Mutual trust needs to be just that. Managers need to trust that their employees know what they are to do, and employees need to feel empowered to engage the resources need to get the job done. While they tout having an open-door policy, most exist on paper only. The most successful companies' policies will be innovative in their endeavors to overcome these self-imposed barriers.

When conflict exists—and it is usually in the top three concerns that employees say need to be resolved—management must address them to remain competitive in the global market. As the baby boomers transition to full retirement from what they currently do, their children (Gen X) will take their place. It's common for existing management to be slow to change philosophies and tap into the talents of this extraordinary generation of new employees.

Senior management people will have to be comfortable supplying one of the most sacred items: their time. The managers will have to show that they just don't give "lip service" ... that they believe in that person's capabilities to achieve the impossible and be willing to help the person get past his/her own skill level. The result: The performance of everyone excels.

Baby Boomer managers must understand what acts as a motivator and what pushes the de-motivator response. Each person has a button and inner drive that must be recognized and built upon. Having the opportunity for individual attention by their managers motivates Gen X. Having access to new tools motivates them. Not only do they want to learn new things, but they also want to receive the acknowledgment of those efforts. And this generation embraces change ... lots of it.

The concepts of delegation will change. The old definition of delegation of responsibility follows comprehensive training and a demonstration that employees can complete the assigned tasks. The new concept flips it. Employees want to demonstrate their independence and ability to do the job with minimal day-to-day supervision. Gen X wants 100% responsibility for the outcome and as they prove themselves give them more. It's the empowerment factor that motivates them. They want to know that you have trust in them ... but if they get into trouble, you are there to get them back on track. You have their back.

Hiring practices will shift from the current concept of hiring the best candidate for the least amount of money, to that of hiring a younger person with three years of experience commanding the same salary as what those accomplished by the management group in 12 or more years. This is a button pusher for the older group. In the past, it was felt that it was only by getting at least two to three years to recoup the cost of training and orientation of new employees before they would contribute to true positive cash flow. The rapid movement and how Gen Xers incorporate their knowledge and skills shatter that belief. It is essential for companies to have a better understanding and adapt their management methods to allow for more motivation and more of a desire for newer and younger employees to stay with the company.

> Do you see a conflict surfacing here?

How Management Will Change

The forward-looking manager must understand the management styles of all generations. In 2022, most executives are of the Baby Boomer generation who place high value on creativity, loyalty, more risk takers, some resistance to new innovations and technologies and are motivated by their perception of appropriate compensation. The next level of managers consist more of the Gen X generation. They display a keen sense of self-reliance, have a natural technical ability, and expect direct answers to questions. They seek work that values their ability and motivates them by challenging assignments and praise. *Do you see a potential conflict surfacing here?*

The barriers that need to be realized include:

- Need to accept that the younger workers move from company to company more frequently.
- Need to be treated as an asset and given responsibilities for projects.
- Need for constant and informal feedback.
- Need for access to methods and a multitude of information.

These concepts are extremely different than how the Baby Boomer managers have been taught over their years of development. They all take time ... something most managers say they don't have more of. Do you see a potential conflict surfacing here?

Each suggestion needs to be examined in further detail as to the expectations and conflicts they will cause. In companies today, most managers expect their younger employees to move to another company within a short time ... that they will job hop. And, that they—the managers—must help them to essentially train for the next job.

This is a direct conflict in how they were brought into the company and believe. Managers normally train those who can be expected to further their careers within the company. Do you mean that I'm supposed to train them to leave ... to advance to another company ... a competitor?

Yes, younger workers do leave. They don't stay in perpetuity. Some HR and recruitment individuals still ask the question:

"What do you see yourself doing ten years from now?" This is as dated as buying a VCR. Don't go there! Instead, know and accept that younger workers are not going to be lifers. Ninety-nine percent will leave. Also understand that they hope to learn more than what they know now. And if they do, they may stay around longer.

What you need to do is:

1. Make training an obsession in your organization. Fill it with various training resources and give the team members the remote capability to use them.

2. Give new project leaders specific objectives and goals and give them the latitude to reach them in their own manner.

> **Trust, while not easily given, is the glue that binds an organization.**

3. Teach by example and how to carve up a project into smaller chucks so they have a functional plan that gives measurable day-to-day results. In a sense, you must teach your virtual workers to micromanage themselves.

4. Embrace constant informal feedback—not the traditional scheduled periodic performance reviews.

5. Communications must be two way and free flowing to be successfully used. The manager will have to be more innovative in the different ways to connect and not to rely on only the verbal methods.

How Not to Manage

Gone will be the yearly performance reviews and replaced with more immediate recognition programs. You will be giving employees more control over setting objectives and goals that will change their creative abilities. Yes, it requires more training resources, but it strengthens the relationship between the leader and your remote employee. The effort would not be in physical resources, but in the personal trust that will need to be extended. Trust, while not easily given, is the glue that binds an organization.

> **Ron's Takeaway**
>
> The old feeling that knowledge is power will have to be discarded. Remote employees will need more access to a much broader and different kind of information. Keep in mind that they grew up in the computer age and are more adept at using different data and technology than many of their senior managers. More resources will have to be authorized to develop the foundation of a much more open company database accessible to many additional levels of workers. This will develop a conflict between confidential information and the need to know but that can be managed by defining the break point in the chain of communications.

Virtual Nuggets

Current US workforce numbers via the Labor Force Composition by Generation Infographic developed by the Pew Research Center:

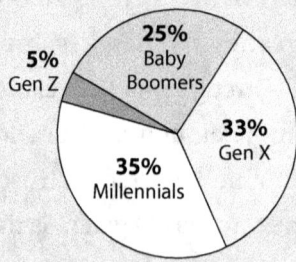

CHAPTER 6

TAPPING INTO THE CREATIVE WELL

To survive in the next decade, companies will require leadership that has the ability to take advantage of any potentially disruptive problem.

Think of the challenges that Kyle must face due to the changes when COVID-19 reared its ugly head. He realizes that he can't do this all on his own, but he has an ace in his back pocket—an entire team of dedicated people like Judy. The key is how to draw out all the essential elements necessary to his team and then encourage that team to come up with new ideas.

The year 2021 saw the need for innovation to lead the way to recovery and growth. It is now a constant requirement for an organization's success. This means that everything that you thought you knew about leadership and virtual leadership needs a magnifying glass look through. Employees, managers, and customers will challenge the status quo of virtual leadership methods that the leadership team and their companies know of today.

Diversity has been a buzzword for several years. Most think that "diversity" is about gender and race. Wrong … it's much more. Let yourself think of diversity as something that cannot merely be managed but needs to be harvested as an ingredient for the creative process. I think of it as a brewing pot of knowledge, experiences, abilities, actions, and willingness brought together. Now, add in the spice ingredients to it all.

- Gender can be a factor;
- Race can be a factor;
- Culture can be a factor;
- Nationality can be a factor;
- Economics can be a factor;
- Upbringing can be a factor;
- Parenting can be a factor;
- Education can be a factor;
- Environment can be a factor;
- Language can be a factor;
- Trauma can be a factor;
- Combat experience can be a factor;
- Political and religious ideologies can be a factor;
- even the state and country one grows up in can be a factor.

And there is always more that can be added to this list. What is the definition of true diversity? It's not just gender … and not just race … but life's experiences brewing in the pot. Depending on the level of the "heat" of any of the ingredients at any time, outcomes are affected. To deal with all the above demands that the virtual leader must be to his or her people, empowering and providing support for them to be successful should be paramount.

To survive in the next decade, companies will require leadership that has the ability to take advantage of any potentially disruptive problem—like COVID-19 that kicked off 2020 with a wrecking ball— and changing it into an opportunity. The company will survive only if its cultural values are true vs fake. For employees, it's not what you say … it's what they see. What's needed is to embrace the idea of using semi-autonomous virtual work teams rather than the more traditional hierarchical arrangement.

> For employees, it's not what you say … it's what they see.

No company was untouched by COVID-19. Granted, some did quite well, being in the right place at the time of the crisis. But a significant number of companies suffered, clawing to survive. Many shut their doors … some forever. With eyes wide open, companies are now faced with rapidly changing business environments.

Welcoming innovation, the result of creative thinking, is imperative. Unfortunately, innovation does not mix well with hierarchy, structure, or closed doors. In fact, the phrase "managing creativity" seems to be an oxymoron. The fabric of corporate management is to control the processes,

> Most companies are aware that their people rarely exceed their creative potential.

while the essence of creativity is that the process be allowed more of a free rein. Mistakes are part of the process. It is evident that the act of institutionalizing creativity takes a lot of work and organizational resources, but it goes deeper than just being able to supply time and money. If employees had unlimited financial resources, the most creative ones would be useless if they did not feel comfortable taking risks. Employees always know if breaking from the status quo brings reward or punishment.

> *The most underutilized resource in most companies is the creative power of its employees.*
> —Dr. Donald Noone, Harvard professor

Ron's Takeaway
As companies move into the new millennium, corporate America will have to take a more serious look at the process of creativity. Why? The answer can be summed up in one word: survival.

Five apps for more creative remote work include:

Brainsparker *https://brainsparker.com/*

Miro *https://miro.com/*

MindMeister *https://www.mindmeister.com/*

Curator *http://curator.co/*

Notability *https://notability.com/*

CHAPTER 7

Group Problem Solving Using Creativity

They embrace innovation as a core strategic driver to their continual growth and survival when economies turn down.

Creative environments will not be possible until it is better understood where creativity can be found and how it can be used effectively in problem solving. Most companies are aware that their people rarely exceed their creative potential. The bigger problem is that they do not know what to do about it. There are solutions and my 40 years as both a manager and leader has embraced problem-solving solutions. My solutions come in steps … there are five of them.

Step 1: *Understanding the Conditions of Group Problem Solving*
Without an understanding of the conditions of creativity, brainstorming, questioning, mind maps, association, analogy, fantasy, relaxation, role-play, or quantum leap thinking, a problem solver will wind up short of reaching the end goal. It will be compounded even more as team activity, with all its

components and complexities, is utilized as a tool for creative thinking. Components include:

- separation and organization of tasks;
- interaction that comes from the exchange of ideas;
- encouragement that comes from having common goals and a healthy competition; and
- a team that can generate more ideas than isolated individuals (most important)

In creative problem solving, there are key impediments that are demonstrated by *impaired* problem solvers. There are inhibiting beliefs, go nowhere questions, impaired instruments, and ignorance of problem-solving techniques.

Donald Noone tells us that there are eight distinct types of impaired problem solvers that can shut down a person's creativity, not only for the individual person but also for the team.

There are the *Dictators, Blamers, Absurdists, Victims, Perfectionists, Jellyfishes, Chameleons,* and *Resisters*.

Dictators believe that idiots, lesser mortals, or folks surrounding them are not endowed with wisdom. The dictator is a master of embracing tunnel vision.

Blamers nothing is ever their fault. Finger pointing is directed at everyone else vs looking in the mirror. Original problem usually gets worse. In organizations, employees hide, receive pressure to lie, and decide it's best to take no risks.

CHAPTER SEVEN: Group Problem Solving Using Creativity 71

Absurdists embrace the irrational, no matter how absurd it is. Immediate response is "it shouldn't have happened!" Absurdists will unleash emotions and pain on themselves and others.

Victims all problems, large or small, are onerous (troublesome). Victims don't understand why they have the troubles but will raise hell over it when they surface. If they complain, then they feel that they are off the hook. Their solution is their moral indignation.

> Perfectionists are the masters of self-sabotage.

Perfectionists the solution must be perfect … always. Perfectionists are the masters of self-sabotage. Human behavior is not perfect. It never has been, nor will it ever be. Human behavior is susceptible to elements that are often uncontrolled. Rarely are solutions good enough for their problems. Perfectionists inflict condemning judgments on themselves, and the golden rule. All energies are tied up in criticism so they don't have much left to solve problems.

Jellyfishes wafflers who are usually on "the line" and are committed to waiting. For them, it is less painful to be neutral. Minimum to slow speed is fine with them, waiting to see what unfolds. Their fear and passivity become their impetus for embracing ideologies, leaders, and groups that claim they do know, and rarely do.

> Rocking the boat that they are in is not where they want to be.

Chameleons usually love to look good. They adapt to fads or the trend of the corporate moment. Chameleons are the professional people pleasers—and most groups have them. Usually inflicted with low self-esteem that they grovel to have someone smile at them, approve of them, or accept them. They never come up with their own solutions to problems. Think of them as the "Yes men and women."

Resisters digging their heels in, they practice the art of hating change, embracing comfort, being routine and always predictable. Committed to the status quo. Deep attachment to order, organization, and the familiar. Comfort is the criterion for a promising idea, not improvement, progress, better service or the greater good of the organization. Resistance is one of the most common syndromes of employees, especially when the dreaded word "change" is in the air. Rocking the boat that they are in is not where they want to be.

Step 2

How to Use Group Creativity

The group creativity process is beginning to receive more attention among the executive ranks. Lack of innovation was seen as one of the largest single problems among corporate executives in research by the McKinsey Research Group. If you look at the companies that really standout as being successful in their industries, it is easy to see that they embrace innovation as a core strategic driver to their continual growth and survival when economies turn down.

There are as many tips on generating group creativity as there are consultants. Everyone has his/her own slant on methods, but the basic concepts are the same ... always. Start with developing a relaxed environment that will empower people to think freely and prepare them to conceive ideas creatively by focusing only on the task at hand.

How does a company cultivate an environment to inspire innovation? A company could easily use six simple tips as starting points in its journey to a more creative environment. They were identified by Dr. Jeffrey N. Shield in his article in the *Association Management Journal* in 1997.

1. Build a foundation for creative planning that encourages group members to be relaxed so they can think freely.

2. Prime the group to think creatively from the start by focusing creative energy on a specific subject other than the task at hand.

3. Employ an icebreaker activity to trigger outside-the-box thinking.

4. Have the group put all open-ended questions unrelated to the problem on the table.

5. Be open to taking risks, which can release the potential for creativity and promote ownership and vision in the group.

6. Break the all-too-common thinking gridlock by asking the group to subscribe to one way of thinking.

As a leader in your organization, you need to support the things that have an influential impact on team members' creativity:

✓ trust

✓ sufficient resources

- ✓ time
- ✓ management encouragement
- ✓ information sharing
- ✓ dedication/commitment
- ✓ personal bond

One of the largest resources that will have to be supplied would be time. Don't cut it short. Studies show that brief time limits lead to lower creativity and feasibility, whereas longer time limits lead to higher creativity and feasibility.

Harvard University Professor Dr. Terese Amabile characterized what stimulates and inhibits the creativity process. They are based on importance.

What stimulates creativity:
- Autonomy in how one does his/her work.
- Good project management determining work assignments.
- Sufficient resources.
- Encouragement.
- Organizational structures that facilitate open communication.
- Feedback and recognition.
- Enough time to do *think time*—3M gives 15% of the week for people to think of new products. In the seventies, 3M scientists Spencer Silver and Art Fry collaborated and produced a clever invention. Fry thought if he could

find a way to apply an adhesive to the back of a piece of paper, it would be a perfect bookmark in his church hymnal. Spencer had the makings of the adhesive. Now known as the must-have Post-it® Notes, a think time allotment that has created more than one BILLION dollars for 3M since inception.

- Google encourages 20% of the week to improve its system. It is how Gmail was created.
- Challenging work.
- Urgent need for a solution, the push of needing it fixed right now.

What inhibits or blocks creativity:
- Infighting or red tape that gets in the way of communications.
- Constraints on what sort of work one can do.
- Apathy toward large projects.
- Unclear project goals and/or too much control over work assignments.
- Performance evaluation pressure.
- Insufficient resources—either equipment or software.
- Insufficient time causing that squeeze of stress in your gut.
- Too much emphasis on standard operating procedures.
- Competition, such as the internal politics within the organization.

Desirable characteristics related to creativity include:
- Self-motivation to achieve something of interest without needing to be pushed by others.
- Special problem-solving ability to identify a problem and determine an effective solution.
- Risk orientation—being comfortable with risky vs certain outcomes.
- Diverse backgrounds to adapt to unforeseen challenges.
- Expertise in the area.
- Social skills to communicate with others.

For true organizational creativity to become an integrated part of your organization, a combination of the creative process, creative product, creative person, creative situation, and how those components interacted together must be in place.

Step 3

Grasping Creativity at the Corporate Level

Corporations get stuck in the old ways. There are elements that are important for promotion of corporate creativity. Think about the necessities of alignment, self-initiated activity, unofficial activity, serendipity, diverse stimuli and internal company communication. How clear are any of those in your organization? Have you asked those you work with on your peer level? What about those who work for you?

Most companies have no to little means to determine where creative acts will occur, but they can take action to increase the frequency in which they can occur. That's where you come in. Think of yourself as the match to light the creativity flame within your team ... your organization.

Alignment is about funneling the interests and actions of the employees toward the company's key goals in such a way that every employee will have the ability to recognize and respond positively to a potentially useful idea.

Self-initiated activity will allow employees to select a problem that they have an interest in and an ability to solve. This means that their intrinsic motivation would be greater if they get to select the project instead of having one assigned to them.

Unofficial activity occurs when there is an absence of official support but there is intent to do something new and useful.

Serendipity in creativity pops up often due to a fortunate accident. Creativity also bubbles up by making connections between unrelated subjects.

- Bathtub and hammock combines into a baby tub. A simple hammock in the tub with a headrest, leaving the parent's hands free wash a, squirmy infant in the water.

- How about sunglasses and windows combining to form the idea of tinted house windows, designed to change colors with ultraviolet light to help keep the house cool. Or how about suntan lotion and insect repellent combining to form a new product, one lotion designed to protect against both the sun and insects.

Diverse stimuli is the result of you having a fresh insight into something that you had already set out to accomplish or a task may have an influence in changing your direction of thought. The "aha" factor. While organizations should do all they can to bring diverse stimuli to their employees, they will probably have limited impact on the results. Companies can't control the results, but they can allow for motivation and opportunity factors for their employees.

> **The key is always: How do they communicate?**

Internal company communication is often murky. While a company has planned activities and defined ways of communications, they may not be ideal. More companies are discovering that the lines of communications are much easier and less formal in small organizations within the company. Some leaders feel that "a company's creative potential increases rapidly with its size." Wrong. Creative potential gets bogged down within larger companies. The key is always: How do they communicate? Does everyone who is listening truly hear what is being said?

Not everyone feels that group creativity is in a company's best interest. Some executives even feel that group activities are a waste of time, energy, and money. While it does take time to learn the methods of brainstorming, the actual results overcome any potential cost implications.

Some believe that individual creativity outperforms that of a group. They feel that individuals working alone will usually develop more and better ideas than the same number of individuals working together as a whole. Data counter this belief. In multiple controlled experiments, group decisions have surpassed the quality of their best individual members' decisions 56% of the time.

Step 4
Gathering the Tools for Group Decision Making

A creative environment delivers a competitive advantage. When combining that with a continuous stream of innovations, long-term corporate performance is sustained.

My forty years of a combo of management and leadership within organizations—large and small—have summed up four essential elements for continual innovation, productivity, and success. Consider:

1. Companies that were more innovative experienced greater performance in growth and profitability.

2. Top leaders who spent more time walking around and interacting in the environment made greater efforts to champion innovation and had more creative and cohesive business units.

3. Sharing a common vision and rewarding innovation, including the mistakes that led up to the new idea or widget, were the most effective means by which leaders could improve the innovativeness of the business units.

4. A significant relationship was found between a leader's openness to change and the extent to which he/she was willing to go beyond just talking … showing by doing.

The leader of the next decade will have to continually find more innovative ways to involve employees in idea generation. To be competitive, companies will need to get extraordinary performance from ordinary employees. It will become more important than ever to be creative, in tapping the potential energy of employees from all levels of the organization. Instead of using the power of their positions—certainly not threats and/or intimidation—to motivate workers, leaders will have to learn methods of using their ideas to inspire. Leaders must create environments that support their employees and allow creativity to flourish.

Step 5
The Role of Leadership of the Past
Several authors see leadership as a key ingredient serving as the link between individual creativity, knowledge, and organizational innovation.

The evolution of management and leadership methods has been on a continual move since the late 1940s when the solution was democratic management. Some people figured out that this was a fake democracy and leadership teams learned that democratic choices were not always profitable.

During the 1950s, the solutions to creative problems seemed to be for a manager to show "consideration" while also controlling task activities. After a while, many surmised that their leader's expression of consideration was illusory.

And during the late 1950s, the solution became Management by Objective (MBO) where corporate management and subordinates negotiated goals for the work to pursue.

Innovation was critical for survival.

The 1960s introduced a new solution: "participative management," where the workforces sent representatives to participate in managerial committees.

Workers felt that managers and leaders were exerting too much influence within these committees and their representatives were gaining their own personal benefits over them.

My management skills took a corporate hiatus in the 1970s ... Vietnam called,

Communications were essential at every level.

and my skills and electronic countermeasures were engaged. The theme of participative management became illusive as military management influence infiltrated organizations.

Back in the corporate organization saddle again, the 1980s new solution became "organizational culture," where organizations were to develop agreement about goals and methods. This was not well received by the workers. The leaders came to the realization that general solidarity did not necessarily mean accomplishing goals and methods.

During the late 1980s, the solution became "quality circles," which expanded in the 1990s into "total quality management."

Now, leap to the 2020s. As the military-influenced leadership phased out, the new generation merged with the older leaving, in some workplaces, five generations under one roof. As technology revamped how work was done and what was not needed, organizations felt like they had been flipped upside down. And COVID-19 and the challenges it created were woven throughout every organization and industry. Size was irrelevant; all were impacted.

Innovation was critical for survival. Communications were essential at every level.

Leadership must change … again.

> **Ron's Takeaway**
>
> The cost of inaction is too high, and the impacts too far reaching to not have innovative leadership in place today. The authoritative/military style of leadership will no longer be effective. Maximizing creativity means fitting work to the talents of the available people.
>
> As companies move into the new millennium, corporate America will have to take a more serious look at such activities as creativity. Why? The answer can be summed up in one word: survival.
>
> It will take strong leadership to find the means to spark the creative minds and tap the full potential of their greatest asset—their employees.

Best Team Collaboration Tools include:

Troop Messenger *https://www.troopmessenger.com/*

Bit.ai/ *https://bit.ai/*

Hypercontext *https://hypercontext.com/*

CHAPTER 8

Building the Foundation for Achievement

Don't just give advice—ask for their ideas.

Kyle felt good about the results, but something was missing in the process. At first, he wasn't sure what the missing ingredient was. Then it dawned on him. His group lacked a method of measuring the progress of its plan as well as a clearly defined way to determine if the group was on the right course.

His question became: How can I engage and motivate my team … a team that has struggled with performance issues?

Let's look at Kyle's team who is struggling and moving toward that ledge of becoming an HR issue. But first, there is Kyle who is also struggling with how to stay on top of his team's many moving parts. It definitely would be easier if Kyle could just drop into someone's office for a quick check. But he and his team are remote and have been for some time. Working virtually with multiple time zones in play has created an environment that has added time and delays in seeing the issues quickly enough.

Judy is also struggling. Her ability to have any life balance was crushed by the COVID-19 impact to her family life. The hours she's been putting in clearly exceeded what she did in her non-virtual work environment. She misses her ability to turn work off and just be home as Mom to her two kids. While she loves her work, there will be a point in which the pressure could push her to find a different job that will release the pressure she's been under.

Mike is still an unknown. His inability to meet deadlines on important assignments and meetings has only gotten worse. Kyle really doesn't know Mike well enough to understand why. What are his issues? Maybe he has a second job? Is it time to cut him loose?

Could Kyle's leadership style be lacking? Is he pushing his team too hard, or maybe … is he too hands off?

What Kyle needs to do is step back … literally, take a deep breath and start with himself. Is there something that he should be providing to his team—as a unit and/or individually—a missing ingredient?

I was raised in the farming country and could relate to Zig Ziglar's story of the water pump. To get the *good water*, you must prime the pump by putting something into it—water. Priming gets the water flowing upward. And when the pumping starts, there is no stopping until the amount of water needed is produced. For the last twenty years, I have had a small water pump in my office to remind me of the value of mentoring and

> **A company needs to take care of its people.**

helping people achieve their goals. I am their primer ... without my support and encouragement, they begin to run dry.

The most successful leaders use more of a coaching style to not only engage with their people but to motivate them. This is much more effective than just telling people what you want and then leaving them to figure out how to do it.

> **People need to take care of the company.**

A company needs to take care of its people and the people need to take care of the company. It is not one or the other, but both must happen.

Leadership expert John C. Maxwell shares:

Leaders must be close enough to relate to others, but far enough ahead to motivate them.

Kyle's stepping back and assessing his own communication and coaching skills led him to the realization that he needed to be the primer of the pump. *I need to be a better coach* became his mantra.

What became of Kyle's bottom line action item? He needed to adapt and expand his coaching skills. He set out to learn strategies and tips that would help him be the best coach he could aspire to be.

Use one-on-one time to discuss person's goals and objectives in life. Discuss what can be done to develop knowledge, skills, and abilities to push him/herself to be a successful contributor. Follow up on each team member's progress toward reaching identified goals. Are your team members moving forward and enjoying a feeling of accomplishment? Or are they becoming frustrated because they are sitting in idle?

Give them tasks and projects that will push them past their current abilities and to support their development goals. If employees feel that they are adding to their resume, they will stay with you. If not, they will bail and find someplace else that will fill that need for growth.

Be honest with constructive feedback to help them improve. You have the knowledge, experience, and capabilities to help them past those speed bumps.

Be specific with expectations. Do the two of you have a real understanding of what is expected? Are projects being worked on that take substantial amounts of time … and not relevant to what is needed for the team … the goal … the company? If so, who's at fault?

That's simple … it's YOU. Somehow, some way, communications took a nosedive. It could be from your side: You were not clear enough. But the employee could also be a player by not asking questions when uncertainty surfaced, or parts of the project being worked on weren't coming together that he or she was responsible for. Help was needed. You needed to know something was amiss, and the employee needed to inform you. But you also need involvement. Tossing one or many people into a project without overseeing and giving input can lead to failure.

Don't just give advice—ask for their ideas. As Stephen Covey wrote in the *7 Habits of Highly Effective People:*

> **Habit 5 is seek first to understand, and then be understood.**

You need to be ready to give feedback that is *not* in a lecture format. This is when "showing" by example highlights the power of coaching. Supporting their ideas and assisting them on identifying the necessary steps they will take for improvement is essential.

Are they moving ahead? Are they stuck? Are they coasting? As their coach, you are helping them not only learn but to keep that forward movement going.

Challenge them to try new ideas. Be careful not to fall into that trap of giving someone a tough time for trying something new, even failing. Use it as a learning experience to share your experience on how they can reach their full potential. Support their efforts; don't throw cold water on them. Every … one … fails. Everyone.

One of my favorite John Maxwell quotes is:

> *The greatest mistake we make*
> *is to live in constant fear that we make one.*

Kyle needs to cultivate Mike and Judy to get buy-in for plans, tasks, and their daily activities. The more buy-in Kyle gets, the more their feelings of ownership push them to take care of the results. *When a company takes care of its people … the people take care of the company.*

Explain the *WHY* for the task or activity. I'm a proponent of the *5 Why* concept of taking it down several layers to help them grasp the value of their efforts, or what can happen if they don't. Birthed from Toyota, it's that "deep dive" that is needed to discover the true root cause of an issue.

Every team faces roadblocks in its daily work. The 5 Whys of questioning can get to the root cause of a problem and protect the process from recurring mistakes and failures.

Reveal examples of where you have seen it be successful. Give them a picture of what success looks like. Visuals often deliver meaningful information that helps them move from the natural path of resistance to one of excitement about achievement. If you have ever watched an ad campaign that evolves around a problem, the visual of the problem combined with the visual of the solution outcome delivers hope and success. Isn't that what you want? Coaches are a combination of kicking people in the butt and cheering them on.

Show them with your words and examples that they are more than small cogs in the wheel. They are a valuable part of what keeps the team successful. Use the "we" more than "you." You may be the lifeguard but both of you are in the water.

Be positive and optimistic. Don't be that person others avoid because your negative views pull everyone down. Don't be surprised to learn that there are people who search for faults like there is an award for discovering them. And you may quite possibly experience a leader who only points out the failures, the things not going well, or items that don't meet his/her expectations.

Kyle needs to ensure that they are motivated and confident to do the work needed, encouraging them to push through when obstacles arise. There will always be obstacles. And be sure to celebrate the successes as they unfold—both small and large.

This is the time to ask questions to understand their world. What could be on their minds? Show them that they are on the team because they are good at what they do. Why do you think I hired you above all the other people?

- What do you like about your job?
- What are the things that aren't your favorite? Typically, these are pushed aside. It's good to know them.
- Who do they talk with when they have questions about work? You or another team member? Some may be afraid of asking you because you may think negatively about them or their work.

Recognize their contributions. I once had a Japanese manager who once told me, "If I don't say you are doing something bad, you must be doing it good." Don't leave it up to them to fill in the blanks. Instead, incorporate words and phrases that bring recognition into their world.

"What I like about your ideas are …."

"You really helped me out when you …."

If you have concerns, be honest. They can tell when you are concerned about them as a person and not just about completing an item on a to-do list.

"I noticed that you aren't as positive as normal. Is there anything that I can do to help?"

"It was unusual that you missed the report deadline. Are you overloaded right now?

"Can I take something off of your plate to make it easier?"

Think about things that you can do to take away an excuse. How about a second monitor? A second one should make it much easier for visibility and productivity. It also shows that you're willing to invest in helping them on stress-creating items. They are looking for what you do, not just what you say.

Be open to offering help or resources. That may mean more time on your part, but it will pay for itself in the long run. Can you help implement a proposed change? Your role is to be the barrier buster.

Clear the road of obstacles in the way of their success.

CHAPTER EIGHT: Building the Foundation for Achievement

> **Ron's Takeaway**
>
> It's easy to confuse your leadership positioning with friendship with and among your employees. You must make hard decisions at times. Friendships can get in the way. It's essential to be fair and consistent. It's critical to be respected ... which means being liked isn't the key to your success in leading your team. Be close to your team. Understand what motivates and inspires each of them. And never forget the power you deliver with two words: thank you. People crave appreciation and acknowledgment. Do it.

Best tools for remote-work culture building include;

https://www.ntaskmanager.com

Go to the website and Search for your tool:

- Task
- Slack
- Basecamp

CHAPTER 9

The Right Tool to Track Performance

If your employees don't buy into the WHY and HOW, your efforts will be sabotaged.

There is the old story of people pushing their way through the jungle, cutting vines, and swatting the ever-stinging Asian tiger mosquito. The team leader had someone climb to the top of a tree to see how far they were from their desired location. The climber reached the top of the jungle canopy and had a clear view of what was ahead. He called down, "Great news, boss. We are making fantastic headway. But ... the bad news is that we are in the wrong jungle!"

Every leader at some time discovers that he or she has landed in the wrong jungle. The success in getting out of it depends upon how quickly it's discovered and measurements for moving forward are put into place.

For Kyle in his workplace jungle, not only must he make sure progress is being made by his team, but that they are supporters of the company's success by pulling in the right direction. What

Kyle is experiencing isn't unusual. It is being playing out in most companies across the country today. Many could go out of business unless they keep their groups pulling toward the goals that will help them be successful in the expanding global market.

- Do the leaders truly know their goals?
- Do the teams truly know their goals?
- Do employees know the goals? Have goals been clearly communicated?
- Does leadership have systems in place to measure the effectiveness of each step?

Many leaders and managers do not have the depth of understanding of the variety and different methods of performance tracking or how to design measurement systems. While the company needs to utilize a solid corporate strategy—deciding the *WHERE*—the leadership team needs to have a matrix measurement scorecard system—monitoring the *HOW*.

Kyle needs a smart, adaptable work group to keep pace in a competitive business world. After all, a company is not a benevolent organization that just loves to give away money to keep people happy. It is critical that every employee understands that what he/she does impacts the company's bottom line and specific, measurable objectives by means of performance tracking creates that connection. It starts with the team member's working environment and the tools that are used. Look at providing things like:

- Internet connections that have an enhanced bandwidth.
- Ergonomic desk and chair.
- Essential workplace lighting.
- A second (or even a third) monitor to improve productivity.
- Computer with video camera or an external camera that can be attached to computer.
- VPN (Virtual Private Network) for internet encryption/security.

The balanced scorecard concept has been used by the corporate world for years in the strategy planning, but COVID-19 has created a need for steering remote organizations in the right direction.

Whether it is in the planning processes or in the method of implementation, both will fail to reach full potential if there isn't a link between compensation and the completion of goals. While in 1992 Robert Kaplan and David Norton introduced the concept for motivating and measuring the performance of an organization using four basic elements: customer, team, innovation and learning, and financial. It's known as the *balanced scorecard*. As a leader, you can now take that very idea to the level that Kyle can use with his remote team ... and for yours.

> There are several areas that need to be managed simultaneously.

Think of the balanced scorecard as your essential indicators, like the indicators in the dashboard within the flight deck of an airplane. In the same way as managing a remote team, there are many complex tasks that provide the pilot with the information needed to fly the plane: fuel levels, air speed, altitude, and bearing. It's no different for you. There are several areas that you need to manage simultaneously in today's complex virtual world. You do not have the time or ability to monitor them all. What you need is the ability to see instantly when something needs your attention.

> **You do not have the time or ability to monitor them all.**

There are four basic elements to a balanced scorecard:

1. How the customer sees your company and team?
2. What must the team be good at?
3. Can you improve what you do and its impact using innovation and learning?
4. Are the financial perspectives under control?

There may be others that are unique to your company. Consider customizing within each element, or adding additional components, for your team and company.

You must be careful not to overload your team. Do it by limiting the number of measures being used and making sure all within the team understand what the measurement is and does and *WHY* it's being done. There was a time when a manager would read a new management book over the weekend and come in

Monday morning with all new measures to track. Talk about information overload. You must focus on a handful of measures that you believe are the most critical.

Let's look at how Kyle could use the tool.

1. How the customer sees your company and team?

    ✓ Percent of customer complaints

    ✓ On-time delivery of services

2. What must the team be good at?

    ✓ Employee skills

    ✓ Productivity

    ✓ Meeting project due dates

    ✓ Attendance

3. Can you improve what you do and its impact using innovation and learning?

    ✓ Customer service excellence

    ✓ Improving operating efficiencies

    ✓ Create more value for customers

4. Are the financial perspectives under control?

    ✓ Mandatory hours for professional development

    ✓ Elective hours for professional development activity

Every industry will have different measures and different definitions of what they mean but the concept is the same. The key is that leaders and managers must select measures that are influenced by employees' actions.

If your employees don't buy into the WHY and HOW, your efforts will be sabotaged.

Put them on a Google document and have the team members update their performance each month. You can't be passive as the leader. You are in the Google docs as much as your team is. It's part of your personal visual measurement so that you remain in "the know" of what the overall team activity is on an ongoing basis. Not only does it provide you with information, but the other team members will also see how the rest of the group is working as well.

Focus on the result, not the work time.

Be willing to invest in your remote team members to help them be productive and satisfied with their job. Consider compressed workweeks such as working ten hours, four days a week. In California, legislators are considering redefining the workweek to four days a week, eight hours per day. Employees are now quick to leave a company to find a "work equals life balance" that they are not willing to give up to return to the office—whether it is remote or brick and mortar.

Recent research indicates that working from home can not only boost productivity, but companies are offering more flexibility for the employees to be successful. Get away from the idea of having to manage when they work or where they work. Instead, concentrate on what is accomplished. Do you really care when they are on the computer or is it more important what they get done? Focus on the result, not the work time.

Look at it to be a way to help your employees remain healthy and on the job. In a 2021 study, the World Health Organization (WHO) found that working an average of 55 hours or more each week increases the risk of stroke by 35% and dying form heart disease by 17% compared to an average 35 to 40-hour. Look how much this could save on the company's health insurance cost. WOW!

Remote leadership and remote teams aren't going away. Forward, they will become the *norm-norm*, not just a temporary solution to what every workplace was thrown into when the pandemic hit. It's like a tidal wave or tsunami … once started, it doesn't get stopped.

As a leader, consider the four D's of remote leadership:
1. Document the issues.
2. Document the discussions.
3. Document the agreements.
4. Document the results.

COVID-19 changed the landscape of where employees (and you) work. The norm-norm is from home for millions. The Genie has been let out of the bottle. Some companies will have blended work—partial physical office time during the week combined with remote. If you think that remote workplaces are temporary, your thinking is wrong. Remote workplaces will be commonplace going forward.

Some leaders and managers don't like the idea. It's time to get over it. If you don't, here's what is coming your way: the good employees will jump ship to another company that will allow working remotely. Do you really want to risk losing your best workers?

Change is inevitable. Growth is optional.
—John C. Maxwell

Ron's Takeaway

Success is like the two sides of a coin: One side is the success of the company, and the other side is the success of the employee. The challenge is to take care of both. Are you up to the task? I believe you are. Prove me right.

Virtual Nuggets

Best resources for employee performance tracking tools include:

Workhuman Conversations *https://www.workhuman.com*

BambooHR *https://www.bamboohr.com/*

intelliHR *https://intellihr.com/*

Culture Amp *https://www.cultureamp.com/*

Lattice *https://ppl.lattice.com/*

ClearCompany *https://offers.clearcompany.com/*

Monday.cm *https://monday.com/*

emPerform *https://employee-performance.com/*

CHAPTER 10

THE PANDEMIC INFLUENCE AND BEYOND

*It's time for new leadership and
management attitudes and methods.*

The rapid changes pushed onto the business world by COVID-19 will be long lasting. Do not think for a moment that they are a passing fad that must be temporarily contended with because you would be wrong. The pandemic has morphed the internal and external landscape of the workplace for the employer ... for the employee ... for the entrepreneur, and for the new quasi-employee that has emerged.

The Great Resignation was first proposed by Professor Anthony Klotz of Texas A&M University in 2020. He predicted that large numbers of people would leave their jobs after the COVID-19 pandemic ended and life returned to normal. Normal is no longer the normal pre-2020 most people long to get back to. It's a new work environment. It's time for new leadership and management attitudes and methods ... and a new workforce.

The pandemic delivered an unexpected gift. The gift is one of change results: management vs micromanagement. If your style is micromanagement, you are now dated and will become obsolete. This is not about work burnout, rather people deciding to take their professional careers into their own hands ... no matter what level their jobs are at.

In September 2021, The US Bureau of Labor Statistics revealed that more than four million Americans quit their jobs, creating an all-time high for those exiting the workplace. You can't afford to disillusion yourself in this rapidly changing *work storm*. If you are still thinking that your old micromanagement style of leadership will work, let me toss some more numbers your way.

The question is ... what's *the more*?

The recommendations that have been offered within *The Virtual Bridge* are supported not only by decades of managerial experience but current research. For example, in September 2021, Ian Cook's *Harvard Business Review* article "Who Is Driving the Great Resignation?" delivered an in-depth analysis of more than nine million employee records drawn from more than 4,000 companies. The palette that was created painted a noticeably clear picture for the virtual leader:

- ✓ Resignation rates are highest among mid-career professionals.
- ✓ The tech and healthcare industries had the highest turnover rates ever.
- ✓ Managers must take a data driven approach to reducing turnover.

CHAPTER TEN: The Pandemic Influence and Beyond

You are in yesteryear if you think that higher pay will ensure loyalty. It doesn't, not today. It's old school thinking and went out the door as the Great Resignation took hold. You can't just throw money at your folks to ensure their loyalty. There must *be more*. The question is ... what's *the more*?

In the first book of the Virtual Nugget Series, *The Virtual Divide*, I looked at the generational issues that a leader must consider, and they are even more critical now. To remind you, the four age generations are broken down by birth year:

Baby Boomers II	1996 – 1964; 54-75 years old
Gen X	1965 – 1980; 39-53 years old
Gen Y/Millennials	1981 – 1996; 24-38 years old
Gen Z	1997 – 2021; 6-23 years old

Typically, I would include the Greatest Generation ... the over 75. Pre COVID-19 changed the retirement stats. Many in the Baby Boomer range have exited the typical workplace, including the entrepreneurial side.

The wide range of generational issues is compounded in that the Gen Yers have been difficult to recruit and even more difficult to retain.

A national survey by *CommericalCafe.com* in March 2021 also indicated that a flexible schedule is more important to Gen Y (Millennials) and Gen X than a higher salary. Recruiting and training a new hire costs thousands of dollars. And it costs thousands of dollars more when you consider the time factor that other employees must pick up to cover the missing employee and the impact on overall productivity. Depending upon the type of work and skills needed, losing a valued employee can cost an employer $10,000 to $100,000.

There still is an attitude that remote workers sluff off on the job. The pandemic forced a rapid transition that quickly axed that supposition. Company after company reported that productivity increased. The *Future of Jobs Report 2020* examined the hybrid working model. More than 78% of business leaders anticipated negative fallout on productivity from remote working during the pandemic.

> It's the hybrid workplace of today.

Those business leaders were wrong. This information is not new. In fact, the *Stanford Quarterly Journal of Economics* article in March 2015 "Does Working from Home *Work*?" revealed that more than 16,000 employees boosted their productivity by 13% within nine months. Some companies reported increased productivity that exceeded 20%. In 2021, Global Workplace Analytics reviewed over 4,000 studies, reports, and articles and found that two-thirds of people want to work from home. In fact, over one-third of them would choose working from home over a pay raise if they had to choose between the two. These combined studies also revealed that:

- 80% of employees consider telework a job perk.
- 14% of Americans have changed jobs to shorten the commute.
- 46% of companies that allow telework say it has reduced attrition.

- 95% of employers say remote work has a high impact on employee retention.

Prudential's series "Pulse of the American Worker Survey" published in March 2021 reported that 42% said that if their job did not offer remote work options, they would go to a company that did. That's significant. And it means that you need to offer it. Granted, not every function can be done remotely. But many can.

As a leader, it's essential for you to get with your management team and identify what can be managed remotely and what must be done on site. It's the hybrid workplace of today. It will become an added item to your job descriptions. Keep your mind open to options to these workplace possibilities. In the Prudential Pulse survey, 68% say that the working remotely option would be ideal.

The More

Yes, it's time to ditch micromanagement. In fact, it's overdue. Your emphasis should be on the tasks being completed vs the amount of time sitting at the desk. Use project management systems that concentrate on tasks that allow you to simultaneously ensure that productivity levels remain consistent. From Peter F. Drucker's introduction of *Management by Objectives* in the mid-1950s, to Six Sigma that was popularized by General Electric's Jack Welch in the 1990s, setting and measuring goals has long been held as the key to good management.

> **Step away from monitoring everything that remote people do. It is a death knell for an organization.**

My personal experience has been successful using measurable goals combined with Objectives and Key Results (OKRs), along with Key Performance Indicators (KPIs) that concentrate on what is accomplished.

Step away from monitoring everything that remote people do. It is a death knell for an organization.

Bringing new blood and vitality to your organization comes with scheduled online meetings, check-ins, and video conferencing to assist your team in bonding.

You must communicate where the company is going, what changes are going on, and how employees will be affected. Fill in the blanks so they don't have to. Otherwise, their proactive minds will, and it could be in a direction that is not your intent.

Finally, get ahead of your competition by prioritizing wellness, especially mental health. According to Deloitte's 2021 "Global Human Capital Trends Report," very few organizations are equipped to deal with their employees' well-being. While most organizations know that it is especially important to their success over the next year and a half, what most do is treat well-being with a benign neglect approach. They hope it will get better by itself or just go away. It doesn't.

> *The greatest danger in times of turbulence*
> *is not the turbulence—*
> *it is to act with yesterday's logic.*
> —Peter F. Drucker

CHAPTER TEN: The Pandemic Influence and Beyond 107

Ron's Takeaway

The new remote workforce will help companies accomplish so much more with less, but you must be willing to adapt your methods.

Become the leader that companies want, what companies need, and what employees are searching for.

If your style is micromanagement, you are now dated and will become obsolete. It's your choice. What do you choose?

CHAPTER 11

My Closing Thoughts

*Your people will look for you to be
the calming agent during the rough times.*

As we come to the end of the second book in the Virtual Nugget Series, my goal was to show you some of the basic skills and elements to help your company, your employees, and yourself be successful without all of the stress that can come with it.

The last two years of having to contend with the challenges created by the global pandemic have set the stage for a paradigm shift in how organizations must be led and managed in a global economy. As a diamond is created under intense pressure, so are your leadership abilities. Think back. What you considered to be stressful is now part of your daily routine … the new normal.

I remember when I first learned how to drive a stick shift many years ago. Push in the clutch with the left foot. Let off the gas pedal with the right foot. Look in the rearview mirror and keep an eye out for other cars. Smoothly shifting the gear, I'd press on the gas again and pray that I would miss the car in front of me. I was so dangerous in those early days. It's all second nature and even calming now. A rhythm that I welcome.

According to a 2009 study by health psychology researcher Phillippa Lally at the University College London, it takes a little more than two months for a person to form a new habit. That same study concluded that it would take an average of 254 days for it to become fully engrained in the user's mind.

Your management style will do the same thing. Your people will look for you to be the calming agent during the rough times.

I was honored to work at Hitachi Computer Products America, Inc., years ago. My time and experiences with Hitachi have flowed through every work environment I've been in since. One of my favorite Japanese presidents took the time to mentor this young manager—me. And one thing has stayed with me over the decades. He told me how I could be like the captain of a large ship. My job would be to keep the ship on course when storms tried to push my ship, and the fleet in other directions. Of course, if the seas were always calm, the ship would not need a captain (me).

The seas are not calm today. Turbulent, chaotic, and confused would be better descriptors.

So today, you must contend with changing market conditions on a global scale, the huge advances in technology and a virus that has brought the world to its knees. What is stressful to you today will be your norm soon ... the new normal.

Your challenge is to take that next step and learn how to understand the strengths of your people. I am here for you. With my books. With my consulting. With my speaking. It's part of my new normal. Let's stay in contact.

—Ron

BOOK THREE OF THE VIRTUAL NUGGETS SERIES

VIRTUAL REMOTE TEAMS

How to Use Scorecarding to Track Performance, and Recognize the Early Warning Signals

CHAPTER 1

The Best Kept Secret in the United States

If a team has similar teamwork strengths, they may tend to concentrate on how to be competitive against each other

What is the difference between being a member of a winning team vs a losing one? In the case of the 2021 Super Bowl game, each member of the winning team will receive $150,000, according to the NFL's Collective Bargaining Agreement. Each member of the losing team will still receive $75,000, which is half the amount that the champions earn. If they only lose by one point, is that fair? Maybe not but that is life in the business world. Everyone remembers the winners but can't name the team that came in second best.

The coaches of the Kansas City Chiefs and the Tampa Bay Buccaneers are all experienced leaders. All the players on the field are the best in their team. So, what is the difference?

The coaches of the winning team use each team member's individual skills and abilities in the right position. They took the time to learn each person's strengths, allowable weaknesses, what role do they perform the best in, and who do they work the best with as a partner.

The same can be found in corporate American, the highest performing teams have the right people in the right team role based on their abilities.

Dr Meredith Belbin, of Cambridge University's Henley Management College in the United Kingdom, studied teamwork for many years, and found that people in teams tend to assume different "team roles." He believes that a team role as "a tendency to behave, contribute and interrelate with others in a particular way," and named nine such team roles that contribute to a team's success.

Understanding Dr. Belbin's Team Roles Model is a fantastic tool for teams that have become unbalanced by havin go too many of the same types of people on the team. Tampa Bay does not have a whole team in which each player is a quarterback. How about if they all had the similar weaknesses? If a team has similar teamwork strengths, instead of cooperating with each other, they may tend to concentrate on how to be competitive against each other.

We will look at the nine different roles of the Belbin Team Role Model, their strengths, allowable weaknesses, and what type of team member do they work the best with.

Everyone in the United States has an understanding of the Myers-Briggs's Type Indicator, but in Europe and Asia, the Belbin Team Role is the management tool of choice.

Get a cup of coffee, sit in your favorite chair, and be prepared for some interesting reading of one of the best kept secrets in the US management system—The Belbin Team Roles.

About Ron Beach

Ron Beach is a speaker, trainer, consultant, professor, and proud United States Marine Corps Veteran.

As the lead faculty for the University of Arizona Global Campus, he conducts classes globally from his office overlooking the third green of his home in Washington or upon occasion from a room on a cruise ship. Dr. Beach believes in staying connected with his team—no matter where he is or where his team members are.

Earning both his master's degree and his PhD in Organization and Management, with an emphasis in Leadership from Capella University, and a Bachelor's in Liberal Studies from the University of Oklahoma, he brings his breadth of over 30 years of corporate experience as the senior director of a US manufacturing company with a billion dollar a year electronic data storage division and was a United States Marine electronic countermeasures technician supporting operations in Laos and Cambodia during the Vietnam War.

Being an organizational sociologist, Dr. Beach is one of a very small number from North America who has traveled to

Cambridge, England, and earned the highly coveted Belbin Team Role Assessment Certification. In 2019, he was honored to become a John Maxwell Team Member.

Ron is the award-winning and bestselling author of *The Virtual Divide*. *The Virtual Bridge* is his second book, and readers can look forward to his third book, *Virtual Remote Teams*, available later this year.

When not working with his remote teams, you might find him scuba diving or a *Quality Matters* reviewer. Spare time finds him pursuing his quest as a Titanic history buff.

He resides in the beautiful state of Washington with his wife Wendy.

How to Work with Ron Beach

Would You Like to Listen … Learn … Be a Stronger Leader?

Ron Beach would be delighted to participate in your Management or Human Resource conference. He is also available to speak to your group or organization. For Virtual Leadership and management consulting, email or call his office. If you want a highly interactive, informative and fun presentation or workshop, call or email him for availability.

Workshops and Keynotes Include:

Virtual Leadership | Belbin Team Roles | Decision Making with Statistics | Corporate Ethics Safety in the Workplace | Japanese Production Systems | Use of Teams and Group Dynamics | Utilizing Project Management International Leadership | Leadership Trends of the Next Decade | Global Supply Chain Management

Consulting by the Hour or by the Project

Information and resources to help your organization with virtual leadership development are available. My blogs and social media accounts are right up your alley in supplying information for today's virtual leader.

Ron is available for in-person and virtual presentations for leaders and remote teams.

Let's get connected:

Ron@RonaldBeach.com

720/202-0141

WEBSITES

RonaldBeach.com

RonaldBeach.info

SOCIAL MEDIA

@DrRonaldBeach

Dr.RonaldBeach

Ronald Beach

Other Books by Ron Beach